A HERO OF JEWISH FREEDOM

A Modern Joseph's Journey from Hijacker to Rabbi

GW00497637

"If any of thine that are dispersed be in the uttermost parts of heaven, from thence will the Lord thy G-d gather thee, and from thence will He fetch thee." (Deuteronomy 30, 4)

In memory of my father, my teacher and rabbi, Rav Moshe Ben Aharon, of Blessed Memory.

We were slaves in the Soviet Union, in the northern land, and Hashem brought us forth from there with a mighty hand and with great wonders. And I am in the Golus (exile).

On my way to freedom I saw miracles, some of them overt and others covert. More than anything, I discovered that each appointed season and festival constitutes a nucleus of time in which the Divine Providence is manifested even more potently.

A HERO OF JEWISH FREEDOM

A Modern Joseph's Journey from Hijacker to Rabbi

RABBI JOSEF MENDELEVICH

Translated by
David Herman

VALLENTINE MITCHELL
LONDON • PORTLAND, OR

First published in 2017 by Vallentine Mitchell

Catalyst House,
720 Centennial Court,
Centennial Park, Elstree WD6 3SY, UK

920 NE 58th Avenue, Suite 300
Portland, Oregon,
97213-3786 USA

www.vmbooks.com

Cover illustration: 'Joseph and his brothers' by
the artist Moshe Hemain © Jerusalem 2008.

British Library Cataloguing in Publication Data:
An entry can be found on request

ISBN 978-1-910383-29-2 (paper)
ISBN 978-1-910383-30-8 (ebook)

Library of Congress Cataloging in Publication Data
An entry can be found on request

Printed by CMP UK (Ltd), Poole, Dorset

Contents

Chapter 1

Turning the Bad into Good

1. THE KADDISH

On the eve of the Destruction of the Holy Temple
In memory of my father Moshe Ben Aharon z'l

I say about myself that I am 'a Pesach Jew', because all of my history is connected with the new Exodus from Egypt from the Soviet Union. I call myself 'a 'Chanukah Jew' because I lit the 'Chanukah candles for the first time when I was still of barmitzvah age. Those candles told me to fight against assimilation. I call myself 'a Purim Jew' because I went out from Gulag to Geula, to Eretz Israel on Purim.

And I call myself 'a Jew of the Holocaust'. I became connected with the Jewish People while working together with Jewish youth in a terrible place for the Jews in Riga during the Holocaust. By the graves of the victims of the Holocaust, their surviving relatives said Kaddish, the memorial prayer.

But the first time that I heard the Kaddish was at the grave of my mother, Chaya Yenta Bat Nechemia Yosef z"l. The cruel Soviet regime took her from us. She left us when I was ten years old. One can imagine a boy, choking with tears, standing in the cemetery beside the grave of his mother and hearing the words of the Kaddish. These words penetrated deep into my soul. The melody and sound of this special prayer enfolded within them the grief of the loss. These sounds rose up high to the highest unknown worlds, and descended, to land down on the fresh grave. I was entranced by the Kaddish, it sounded like a song of sorrow of the whole of Israel for the thousands of years of exile. Then I made a vow to myself, that when I grew up, I would know how to say the Kaddish. Thus I became 'a Kaddish Jew'.

In the underground movement I learned a little Hebrew, and I already knew how to say the Kaddish by heart. I began to attend the synagogue in Riga. This decision to attend the synagogue as a young boy in the Soviet Union was an act of daring. My contemporaries said that I was a fanatic. I wasn't a fanatic. But I made it my goal to go to the synagogue and to learn to pray. In the synagogue I again heard the Kaddish. I didn't quite understand why they said Kaddish when there was no grave, but I noticed that at the end of the Shacharit morning prayer they said the Kaddish many times. The morning prayer ended with the Kaddish. I came to the conclusion that, after everything that was holy, they recited the Kaddish.

This was not a correct understanding, but no one in the synagogue was prepared to explain to me the meaning of the prayer. There were there old people who knew the Soviet law. According to the Soviet law, whoever taught Judaism would be sentenced to five years in jail. And perhaps in my conclusion, that something good ended with the saying of the Kaddish, there was an element of truth.

When I was in Chistopol Prison I was in the same building as Natan Sharansky. We were able to converse by means of the prisoners' 'telephone', the waste pipes that connected toilet bowl with toilet bowl in each cell. About this special connection I shall tell later. One day I heard 'over the telephone' the choking voice of Anatoly (this was his name before he immigrated to Israel) – 'Yosef, my father has died.' I felt a deep sorrow in my heart. How could I help my friend? Suddenly I knew- I would send him a Kaddish! I at once wrote the words of the Kaddish on a piece of paper and took it with me 'on an outing'.

One must explain that in the West all the prisoners go for a walk in the courtyard together, but we belonged in the category of 'very dangerous security prisoner' and so they didn't allow us to go out together. The courtyard was divided up into triangles and between each of the triangles there were partitions so that we could not see or speak with one another. But the prisoner is always cleverer than the warder. In primitive Russia the partitions were made of wooden planks and in the planks there were holes. Overhead there was a net so that we could not throw letters to one another. And above all of this monstrosity the warders walked around and kept an eye on us. Apparently, there was no way to transfer the Kaddish. But I had a plan. I made my Kaddish into a small paper ball and hoped to be able to throw it up in the space between the nets. The net was very narrow, and the chance of throwing accurately so that my Kaddish would pass from my side to Anatoly's side was very slim. But hope warms the heart.

Every time they took me out for walk, I would immediately whisper in the direction of the adjoining courtyard 'Who is there?' And if it was Anatoly I would whisper – 'Get ready. I am sending you the Kaddish prayer.' He was ready and tense – not to miss the 'delivery'.

'I'm throwing!'

Everything was against me. The narrow net made it almost impossible to hit the opening between net and net. Overhead, the warders walked around on the lookout for the very thing which I wanted to achieve. I waited for the warder to come to where I was, and the moment that he turned his back to retrace his steps, I would try to throw the ball and succeed in my mission. This continued time after time.

'I'm throwing!'

I failed. The following day and the next I threw and again I failed. His Shiva (the 7-day period of mourning) was nearing its end and I still hadn't succeeded in delivering the Kaddish. I was almost in despair. The last day:

'I'm throwing!'

And suddenly I hear Anatoly's voice – 'I got it!' I can't recall a day when I was so happy. I went back to my cell and wept with emotion. I had helped my friend!

The day came when my father also passed away. He was very ill. The doctors told him that perhaps only in Israel could the doctors cure him. But Father refused to leave the Soviet Union. 'As long as my son is in prison, I shall not leave him.' He sacrificed his life for me.

As it says about Joseph and Benjamin in the Book of Genesis, 'His soul is bound up with the lad's soul.' His heart failed and he passed away. He died on the eve of the fast of the 17th Tammuz. They didn't inform me – 'in order not to cause extreme emotion to the prisoner.'

My father died in the Diaspora but, due to the intervention of President Nixon, the Soviet authorities permitted him to be brought to Eretz Israel for burial on the night of the 9th of Av. I did not know the day of his death. But, in any case, I was fasting in memory of the Destruction. And so, also on Tisha B'Av, the day of mourning for the Destruction of the Temple, by participating in the national mourning, I was enabled to observe my own private mourning.

After a long while, the fact of my father's death was revealed to me by chance. I didn't know how to react. I sat on the floor of my cell and fasted. I wanted to say Kaddish. I knew that one said Kaddish only with a Minyan, a quorum of ten men There was no Minyan in the cell; there were six people, Ukrainians, Armenians, Russians. But, nonetheless, I recited the Kaddish. I added to my grief that of the victims of the Great Revolt at the time of the Destruction and that of all the members of my family murdered in the Holocaust. Thus, I had much more than a Minyan. I spoke to them and they answered me. 'Yitgadal ve'yitkadash shemei raba...'

2. MERIT OF THE FATHERS

Everything that has happened to me in my life came about as a result of General Providence and as a result of Divine Providence. I often ask myself why it was that these miracles happened to me of all people. Apparently, it was due to the merit of my forebears, and the last of them was my father and teacher, Rabbi Moshe Ben Aharon.

At the time of the Soviet conquest my father worked in the municipality of Dvinsk in Latvia. Dvinsk was a large town which produced such great Torah scholars as Rabbi Meir Simcha of Dvinsk who wrote the 'Meshech Chochma' ('The Price of Wisdom') on the Torah, and the Rogatchover Gaon , Rabbi Yosef Rosin. My father's function in the municipality was to find housing solutions for needy families. In actual fact, his job was to place families living in overcrowded conditions in villas and private houses of well-to-do people and thus to squeeze out the legitimate tenants.

Once, Father received an order to transfer a poor family to a more spacious apartment. Upon arriving there, he discovered that the Soviet municipal officials intended, on the pretence of providing the poor with a housing solution, to eject from the apartment the family of the Rabbi Meir Simcha of Dvinsk (he himself had long since passed away). To harm the family of a great Jewish scholar? No! Father disobeyed the command even though he was well aware how this would anger the gentiles who hated the Torah. The family of Rabbi Simcha remained in its apartment.

Very shortly after this, the Germans, may their name be blotted out!, reached the outskirts of Dvinsk. The Jews didn't know what awaited them, and didn't want to run away and leave their homes. So they remained and were condemned to a terrible massacre. But my father, may his memory be blessed, knew that, since he was a Soviet municipality employee, the Germans would have no mercy on him, and so only one option was open to him – flight. In the municipality there were two heaven-sent carts and horses. On one cart travelled Father, Mother and my older sister Rachel of Blessed memory. On the second cart were my mother's sister, Pessia Devorah, with her sons. At least a part of my family was saved.

Divine Providence wished to reward my father twice. Why just Father and why twice, I am not sure, but it is a fact that when I was an adolescent there was sent to live with us Dr Menachem Gordin, may the Lord preserve him, the younger son of Aunt Pessia. This young son who was already a grown man, infused in me love of the Land of Israel and the Torah.

Thus, thanks to Rabbi Meir Simcha of Dvinsk, may his merit protect us, I came to Torah, to Mitzvot and to Eretz Israel.

3. YOSEF MENDELEVICH REMEMBERS STALIN'S DEATH (PURIM, 1 MARCH 1953)

I also remember the day that Stalin died. We were living in Riga, a city captured by the Red Army only a few years earlier. I was six years old. and was playing with friends in the courtyard. They were Russians and Latvians. There were no Jews, since most of them had perished in the Holocaust. Suddenly a mood of deep gloom descended on the city. I sensed that something had happened.

I went up to our apartment on the third floor. The apartment was in darkness. Someone had turned off the electricity. I entered one of the rooms. What's this? My mother was sitting on the floor. In her hand she was holding a newspaper with a large picture of Stalin. My mother was sobbing, sobbing. 'What's the matter, Mamele?' I asked in alarm. 'Stalin has died!' answered my mother tearfully. 'How shall we live without him?' The war had only recently ended, and we were all convinced that we had been saved thanks to Stalin. The paradox was that Mother's brother, Dov Ber Berkovitz, had been killed with his wife in 1937 by Stalin, and their little son, who had been named after the founder of the KGB, Felix Dzerzhinsky, had been taken to an orphanage of the 'enemies of the people'. My uncle, Dov Ber, was one of the heads of the Communist Party in Latvia, and fled from there to the Soviet 'Paradise' where he was killed.

Despite Stalin's death, for us ordinary folk nothing changed in our lives. We were still living in the shadow of 'Father Stalin'. Only in the 1960s did rumours begin to surface about Stalin's crimes. But even now many citizens continue to admire him. Nevertheless, the Soviet regime without Stalin gradually weakened. It is impossible to keep people in subjugation without cruel means of oppression. It was the beginning of the end for the regime, but its death throes lasted another 35 years. The readiness of an entire nation to believe in 'the Sun of the Nations' and to ignore his crimes and lies, teaches us a depressing lesson about human nature. This we have to remember.

It is also a Mitzvah to remember 'what Amalek did to you'. To my mind, also remembering the stupidity of people who believed in the 'progressive' lying slogans of Communism – is part of the observance of this Mitzvah.

I also remember ....a few years earlier...

The atmosphere in the city was very tense. It was cold and gray. Once I went with father to a supermarket. Suddenly two Russian officers in long military coats stopped Father. I was a small boy and so the officers seemed to me to be very tall. Menacing us. One of them said to Father in a hostile tone of voice-

'Show your documents.'

Father asked 'Why?'

And the officer said – 'Your face looks suspicious to me.'

They examined Father's documents for a long time. It was clear that he was in danger. But Father was calm, and I also was not afraid. Finally they returned Father's passport. The experience was so traumatic that I remember it to this day.

As you know, before he died Stalin accused the Jews of being enemies of the Russian people. He intended to send us all to Siberia so that we should perish there from the cold and hunger. Nevertheless, the Soviet citizens underwent an intensive brainwashing, and for them Stalin the tyrant and murderer was like a holy deity. At that time I was six years old....

4. TURNING THE BAD INTO GOOD – IT ALL DEPENDS ON YOU!

There is something sad about the sequence of the festivals – Rosh Hashanah, Yom Kippur and Sukkot. After all, we are in the transition from summer to autumn and winter. Nature is no longer in bloom. It has fallen asleep in anticipation of the renewal of spring. And we are bidden to rejoice – 'Rejoice in your festivals and be happy!' And perhaps the command to rejoice comes like an order, so that despite the sadness we must be happy. Here the Torah teaches us that the life rhythm of the People of Israel does not belong to the natural process. Nature has gone to sleep whereas the People of Israel awake to a new life and to new plans: 'Shana Tova! A good year, a year of renewal!' Thus do we greet our fellow men. I think that the aforementioned contrast can help to explain the saying of the Sages that, under certain circumstances, 'the vices of the penitent are accounted as virtues'.

Basically, the saying means that if you feel remorse and contrition after committing a bad act and the determination to never repeat the mistake – this means that the bad action has led you to reform and repentance, thereby, in retrospect turning the bad action into something good. This can also apply when bad things happen to us.

In my lifetime I have experienced several major events which happened to me during the festivals. It seems to me that if I relate them you will see how the principle I spoke about works – to turn the bad event into something good. To begin with, I will tell you about my first Rosh Hashanah.

I was born after the Second World War in Riga, the capital of Latvia, which was conquered by the Russians. My childhood was not an easy one. In 1957, when I was ten, my father, Moshe Mendelevich was arrested by the police in the course of the Soviet regime's persecution of the Jews. (This was already after Stalin, in the days of Khruschev.) This was a tragedy for my family. My mother could not take it. She fell ill and subsequently passed away. When my father was released ill from prison, I decided to go and work in order to help my father financially. You can imagine what happens to a Jewish child who comes to work in a Russian factory – around him are drunkenness, lawlessness and moral corruption. Nothing of the dirt of that life clung to me.

In the evenings I went to evening classes to finish my high school studies and begin my university education. I suddenly discovered that

Five years old in Riga, Latvia. 1952.

Working Youth School No. 25 was special as it was attended by a large
number of Jewish boys. In my previous school I had got used to the
fact that there were very few Jews, perhaps a single one in each class.
And so I had always felt myself to be in the minority. But in this school,
and especially in my class, the majority were Jews. I felt myself very
much at ease. Among us were friends who were closer to Jewish
tradition. Once, during the break, one of the boys, Lev Levinson, strode
to the front of the class and announced:

'Today is the festival of the New Year, no lessons!'

'Which new year?' I asked. 'The new year begins on the first of
January and now it's the middle of September!'

'It is the Jewish New Year,' Lev explained.

'What a strange custom! Unlike the rest of humanity.'

But we had no choice, all the Jewish classmates began to leave the
class.

'Where are you going?'

'To the synagogue.'

'What!? What are we going to do in a synagogue, we belong to the
new generation, people of science and technology, and a synagogue –
that's a place for senior citizens.'

What to do? I didn't want to be left alone, so I reluctantly went
with all the rest. Actually we didn't enter the synagogue. We remained
in the courtyard and in the adjacent street where there were already
many Jews, as well as young boys and girls of our age. It was pleasant.
So much so that I asked Levinson:

'Is there any other festival coming soon?'

'Definitely – in nine days' time.'

I didn't know that this was Yom Kippur. I didn't care what festival.
The main thing was that I would once again be able to be in the
company of my new friends.

And so for the first time I came to synagogue on Rosh Hashanah.
Quite possibly, if my family had not known tragedy, perhaps I would
not have come so quickly to a synagogue. I have to note that then, in
1963, Zionist activists decided to exploit the official standing of the
synagogue in order to establish a semi-legal meeting place for youth
and to set up on this basis an underground Zionist movement. And this
was indeed what happened.

After Rosh Hashanah came Yom Kippur. The Yom Kippur about
which I wish to relate took place six years after the first encounter with
Rosh Hashanah. I was 22 then, and one of the leading activists in the
Jewish underground in the Soviet Union, the editor of the nationwide

underground magazine. And something else occurred. Since there was no opportunity of emigrating to Israel, I decided with a group of friends to hijack a Soviet aircraft and flee to Israel. We hoped that this exceptional act would attract the attention of the Jewish world to our plight, and enable the lifting of the Iron Curtain to permit free emigration from the Soviet Union.

We were unsuccessful. We were arrested. They attempted to break our spirit and make us cooperate with the regime. I was not broken, and so one day they transferred me to a mental hospital called 'Serbski' in central Moscow. This was a KGB facility. If someone was dissatisfied with the situation in the Soviet Union- he must surely be crazy! Because every normal Soviet citizen had to love Communism.

For my first 'medical' visit there came to see me a colonel of the KGB with a white gown over his shoulders. He said to me at once: 'If you cooperate, you will go back to prison, if not - we shall register you as being a mental case and will give you special drug treatment.' Some time later they brought me for examination to the chief psychiatrist, Professor Daniel Luntz. He sat on a tall chair, as if on a throne. Around him were – doctors. I saw Jewish faces. They were enjoying the show.'What!? You wanted to be the King Messiah?' the professor asked me. He spoke the words in the Hebrew tongue. Apparently, he had once studied in a yeshiva before the Bolshevik Revolution. I understood that they wanted to accuse me of megalomania.'No, I am a simple man and we have family in Israel, therefore I wanted to be with them.' The answer did not satisfy him, and he continued to ask me all kinds of trick questions.

After they took me back to my cell I was very disturbed. What would they do with me, would they really begin to give me injections to make me go out of my mind? There were there some patients who had already undergone the 'treatment'. It was terrible.

A few days later Professor Luntz summoned me again. This time he was alone. 'Young man, you have a problem. Do you think that I can help you?' The question was unexpected. I hesitated about what to say. Apparently, he wanted me to ask him to pass a letter to my friends and thereby to trap me. But perhaps he really did want to help me? Perhaps he felt sorry for a young Jewish boy? Suddenly there sprang into my head an evasive answer: 'I don't know, perhaps you can help me. I only ask one thing of you- don't harm me.' He replied, 'Is that all you are asking for?' He was silent for a moment – 'OK.' He pressed a button and a policeman arrived to take me back to my cell. I was extremely stressed, and felt that at any moment I would go out of my mind.

After a month of tension there came a young KGB lieutenant and said that I was leaving the 'hospital'. 'Where are you taking me?', I asked. I knew that in Moscow itself they didn't do the forced 'treatment'. Apparently, they were taking me to some secret facility to continue the torture. But the young lieutenant said: 'Professor Luntz, who is a big expert, decided that you are pretending to be a mental case in order to evade the trial. But the truth is that you are well and able to stand trial. Therefore, we are returning you back to the prison to continue the interrogations.' What good fortune, what happiness! I will be on trial with my friends. I prefer to be given the death sentence rather than to remain in the asylum.

My luck didn't end there. Instead of loading me onto the prison train, the lieutenant took me to a regular train, and I could for a moment imagine that I was a free man. During the journey the young officer asked me whether I was perhaps hungry: 'I have some apples here.' And he took out two fine apples the like of which I hadn't seen in the prison.

I must emphasize that before the plane hijacking attempt I had learned by heart some dates of the Jewish festivals. That date was the last one that I remembered – it was the eve of Yom Kippur! Those apples reminded me of the apple with honey we eat on Rosh Hashanah. Did the KGB officer know about the festivals of Israel? He took out a book- 'Perhaps you want to read?' I looked. It was Leon Feuchtwanger's *The Jewish War*,' about the great revolt against Rome. I almost felt that they had sent Elijah the Prophet to me.

We believe that on the eve of Rosh Hashanah two books open - for life and for death, and on Yom Kippur they are signed. I don't know for which book I was inscribed on that Yom Kippur. Perhaps it was for a third book, a book of hope. At the trial, the People's representatives demanded the death penalty for me and my comrades. But through international pressure, which the Russians hadn't anticipated, they annulled all the death sentences and mitigated them. I got 'only' 12 years imprisonment in a forced labour institution.

After Yom Kippur comes the festival of Sukkot. In the forced labour camp I tried very hard to observe the Mitzvot – Shabbat, prayer, festivals – even though for everything I was punished. I spent three years in the harsh conditions of the closed prison for observing the Shabbat. Only one Mitzvah I was unable to keep – the Mitzvah of Sukkah. Who was going to permit me to build a Sukkah in a KGB camp!

Some years later, I saw at the edge of the camp a pile of straw. I knew that if I could scrape the straw so that I would from underneath

1957, the year in which my father was arrested and my mother died. Last moments of happiness in Riga, Latvia. Mother, Father, my sisters and me. (In the background is the Academy of the Arts building.)

be able to see the stars – this would be considered as observing the mitzvah of Sukkah. The problem was that this pile of straw was near to the camp's electric fence . It was forbidden to approach it. One might be suspected of an escape attempt and be shot at. But the desire to observe the mitzvah overcame the fear. Towards evening, when they had not yet lit the projectors on the guard towers, under cover of the darkness, I ran toward the pile of straw, got inside it, scraped the straw, looked at the stars and made the blessing 'who has sanctified us by Thy commandments, and hast commanded us to dwell in the Sukkah'. As soon as I finished the blessing, I rapidly retreated from the Sukkah. But my heart was filled with joy. I did it!

Thus, from that first miserable Rosh Hashanah of the start of the long trek, I had reached the Sukkot of confidence and faith. Shortly thereafter I was released and went straight from the prison 'expelled' to Israel.

It seems to me that this story exemplifies how, despite the sadness of the approaching winter, a Jew can rejoice and create his own world of struggle within himself and victory – in the end it all depends on you!

Evening of Jewish music with friends in the Riga Jewish underground, 1968.

Chapter 2

Genesis

5. THE DECLARATION

I wrote this document a day before our operation. I suddenly felt that they could kill us and nobody would know what had happened to us. I understood that something in the nature of a will must be left behind.

I searched for some verse that would express our intentions. I took the Bible, opened it, and immediately saw the verses of the Prophet Zechariah. Now I knew that we were obeying the command of Hashem.

1 Sivan 5730 (1970)

'Ho,ho, flee then from the land of the north, saith the Lord…Ho, Zion, escape…'
(Zechariah 2 – 10,11)

We, ten Jews, living within the territory of the Soviet Union, are determined to take a daring step in order to leave this state. We shall no longer plead with the Russian authorities to be allowed to leave their state

We are an integral part of those hundreds of thousands of Jews who, for decades already, have been declaring their desire to emigrate to Eretz Israel.

Despite all these repeated requests, the Russian authorities refuse to acknowledge this basic right of ours.

The refusal of the Soviet authorities to allow us to leave their state, constitutes a severe violation of international law and of a basic human right. The Soviet authorities are well aware that they are also acting in violation of their own constitution. Nevertheless, they invent all kinds of strange excuses to prevent us from emigrating to Eretz Israel.

The government officials tell us brazenly that in our lifetimes we shall not see Israel and that we shall rot in Russia.

Every Jew who declares his desire to emigrate to Israel is treated badly and persecuted, and many are sent to prison. In Russia they treat the Jewish minority like an alien body. As we know, in the days of Stalin the Jewish community here was in danger of annihilation. Although the Stalinist tyranny has passed from the world, the danger of annihilation still hovers in the air. In the very best case, it has been decreed that we should vanish as a nation under the weight of enforced assimilation.

The Soviet authorities have declared that they are 'close to a final solution of the Jewish problem'. Such declarations are laughable. They could only solve the Jewish problem by anti-Semitism, discrimination and forcible assimilation. They must not be allowed to decide our fate. The sole viable solution for us is - to return to our native land, which is Eretz Israel.

We appeal to the United Nations and to all free peoples: you must put an end to the inhuman attitude to the members of our nation, otherwise you have no right whatsoever to speak in the name of humanity.

Unfortunately, we have experienced at first-hand the apathy of the world which stood by indifferently when the blood of our people was shed.

We are appealing to Jews throughout the world. It is your duty to make every effort possible to save the Jews of the Soviet Union. Our fate is in your hands - to survive or to vanish.

We are thirsty for freedom and want to enjoy all the goodness which the modern world can provide. You who are enjoying this goodness must use all the means available in the free society in order to defend our natural rights.

So long as we are denied the right to be in Israel, you must build our Jewish home and make good our absence.

My brothers, please, if we don't succeed in our mission, our relatives will be exposed to persecution by the cruel regime. Please, take care of our family members and protect them.

N.B. We must emphasize that our action involves no danger for anyone. In the plane there are no passengers, apart from our group which is escaping in order to save our People.

The undersigned:

Yosef Mendelevich, Edward Kuznetsov, Mark Dimshytz, Israel Zalmanson, Zeev-Wolf Zalmanson, Silva Zalmanson, Meri Mendelevich Khnokh, Arieh Khnokh, Anatoly Altman, Boris Penson

6. THE FESTIVAL OF SHAVUOT

The Midrash says that the verse 'go forth o ye daughters of Zion, and gaze upon King Solomon, even upon the crown wherewith his mother hath crowned him in the day of his wedding, and in the day of the gladness of his heart', is talking about the Revelation at Mount Sinai, which is like a wedding covenant between the Nation of Israel and Hashem.

There were ten of us, aged between twenty and thirty, and we were trying to escape from a northern land to Eretz Israel, our natural dwelling place. We were unaware of this significance of the term 'wedding', and purely by chance we called our escape operation 'Operation Wedding'. We planned to hijack a plane in which we would fly to Israel, piloted by one of the members of the group, a professional pilot. The exact date for the hijacking was set for the Sunday, a day when we were free from work, which was also the day of elections to the Supreme Soviet. We assumed that, because of the holiday, the level of alertness of the security arms would be low, and also because it was to be expected that on such a day most of the policemen and soldiers would be drunk. Fate decreed that the date was changed to a different day, to 11 Sivan 5730 (15 June 1970), which fell within the week of the Festival of the Giving of the Torah, Shavuot.

It was fitting that the sons of Israel, who had considered redeeming the people of Israel from the land of exile, should protect themselves by the merit of the Giving of the Torah when the Jews had placed the 'we shall do' before 'we shall hear'. Here too, readiness and great faith were required.

On 11 Sivan, the ten of us set out, ten Jews, on our way to make a wedding contract with Israel, with its People, its Land and its Torah, intending to land within a few hours in our Holy Land. The thought of this choked my throat with excitement. Perhaps, who knows?

But in vain.

Within a few hours I was already imprisoned in a narrow cell, lying on a straw mattress and asking myself if I would be able to withstand this test. Where would I find the strength?

I remembered the heroes of Israel who sacrificed themselves for what they believed in. 'But I am not a hero. I don't want all of this. I want to live.' And again the question arose – how will I be able to? Since I did not have an answer, I felt enveloped in loneliness and sealed from any connection with Hashem. I didn't have the strength to be uplifted, and only there arose in me an unconscious prayer: 'Please, Hashem, please save me!'

And He did.

One day I awoke in the morning with a new thought in my heart: 'Why am I in despair? Everything will be alright. I don't know yet how, but I am sure that things will turn out right. Everything which we did – we didn't do for ourselves, and so there is no need to be afraid.'

Thus did I gain confidence in Hashem, and since then I knew that the question 'will I be able?' was a suggestion of the evil inclination, and the evil inclination is the Angel of Death. From now on, I knew that I would recite a new verse: 'With Hashem's help we shall be able.'

'From the deeps I have called to Thee, Hashem'.

Chapter 3

Life as a Prayer

7. A BOY'S PRAYER

A rainy winter's day in Latvia. I, an eleven-year-old boy, am standing with my sisters opposite the court building. Inside the big building is Father. The police state is judging my father. They are accusing him with vain accusations: 'Dereliction of duty.' Jews are always guilty.

Gray and cold. We have nothing to look forward to. The very building itself exudes cold But somewhere inside me a thought arises. Where is that? Inside my heart? In the chest? I don't know the word 'soul'. I also don't know the word 'faith'. Not yet. There, inside me, I whisper: 'Only cause Father to be released.' Do it, I ask with all my strength. Who am I asking? Who had taught me to ask for something coming from there, from inside me? What is this? A prayer. What else if not a prayer?

Under pressure, with a tremendous effort, while summoning up all his being, an eleven-year-old boy says: 'Only do it.' What then? What will be? I don't know, I only request, only believe that if I will ask correctly, with all my might, He – the one to whom I am making the request - will be able to help. Even if it impossible. I am asking for a miracle to occur, only a miracle. And, in fact, the miracle did occur. Within a year Father was free. But too late. The family was already destroyed, and Mother was gone.

Nonetheless, perhaps I had been answered after all. Because, through my prayer the path to Heaven had been opened to me.

8. THE SECOND TEST

I am already a young man, studying in university and searching for my way. My head and most of me are in Eretz Israel, and I am still in the

East. I have to take a physics exam and I don't have the strength. Why must I study at a university in Riga instead of making my way to Eretz Israel?

And then, as if of its own accord, there came to my mind a book in the Holy Tongue, the Book of Joshua, which I had inherited from my grandfather, Nehemiah Yosef. The book is lying there in a cupboard, and in my view it is very special. It contains things that I do not understand, but I feel I know that they contain a secret, and if I will read them they will help me. My parents had already taught me the Alef Bet (the Hebrew alphabet) in my childhood.

I rummage in the cupboard, identify the book and pick it up. I read it. Even though I don't understand the words, I am intoxicated by the melody of the words. I cry out with enthusiasm. I call to someone: 'Please save me.' And I know that He will save me.

* * *

Several more years have passed, and again I find myself at a crossroads. I decide to escape from the worn path of routine. I leave this world, this grayish, base world. I disconnect myself and I go to Eretz Israel. How? I don't know. The main thing is to set out on the way to the future and to leave the past. I decide to leave my work and university studies. This is not a logical decision, it is a flight. From where to flee is clear to me, but to where?

And then came the call-up to the Soviet Army. The darkness of hell menaces me. And all at once there came to me the simple realization. Now I have to decide. I had known this for a long time, but I wanted to ignore it. There is one simple truth. I have to serve Hashem. For a long time I have known this inwardly but attempted to disregard it. Today, I cannot escape from it any longer. If I want to save myself, I swear to You, Hashem, that from today on I shall be a Jew as you require of me.

They send me from the Army for a psychiatric observation. And the medical committee decrees: 'Sane, but problematic. He must be exempted from army service.' I am saved! From now on I begin to keep my vow. On Shabbat I walk through the whole city to the synagogue, to the long prayer service recited in the Ashkenazi style. I sit amongst elderly worshippers. I don't understand; I listen and am bored. But I have to keep my promise, although I have no idea at all how to be a Jew.

Long months pass. The Jewish underground, which I belong to, involves us in a heavy load of activity. The decision I had made is all but forgotten.

9. THE THIRD TEST

I am already in prison. I tried to escape to Eretz Israel and I was caught. I am by myself in a cell, and every day they call me for interrogation, At first I had to face a brutal interrogator. Shouting, threatening. I was afraid. Perhaps the death sentence would follow, or life imprisonment. But the uncertainty is even worse than the fear. There is nothing in view. As if life has ended. It's all over.

They change the interrogator. The new one is bespectacled, speaks quietly, smiles.

'What happened to you, Yosef? I don't understand. You are like me. After all, you belong to our Soviet nation. You speak like us, you look like any other Russian. Don't worry, we understand your situation. We will help you. Only don't be so stubborn.'

See, there is hope. Perhaps they will have mercy on me. Perhaps I will remain alive. A person needs a little hope. I want to live. I really want to live. To live? Like a gentile? Like a dog? Without hope? Without a name? Where shall I find the strength to save myself from myself?

In the background, the KGB building in Riga where I was held in the basement below ground, 1970.

I thought to myself: 'I really do understand him, I understand his language. And really, why does he say that I don't look a Jew? That I don't act like a Jew? Oy, if only I didn't understand Russian. If only I lived in another world of thoughts. My own thoughts. Not theirs. How to escape from this mire which the interrogator is sticking me in?'

I - like him?

The answer is clear to me. Be different. If I will be a Jew I will not be like them. To be a Jew is to act like a Jew, and what distinguishes the Jew from the others is keeping the Mitzvot. If I observe the Mitzvot, he will understand that I am 'lost' to him, that I am not like him, that I am different.

How does one observe the Mitzvot? One covers one's head, and if there is no kippa headcovering, even with a rag. And is there more? Well, yes there is. One must pray. A Jew prays. Already in the past I had vowed to Hashem that I would pray, and why hadn't I prayed all this time? Because they hadn't taught me how to pray. In a moment of clarity I recalled how I had prayed before the trial. Yes, that was a prayer. I remembered it ever since then.

Yes, one must pray. I want to pray. My heart prays all the time. Only to tell, to recite, to read. I read about a little boy who didn't know how to pray, and threw the twenty-two letters of the Alef Bet in the air. I know Hebrew, I can write the prayer. And I also remember that the Jews, so I have read, don't pray for themselves and their welfare only. The prayer recited by a Jew must be for all of Israel, and afterwards he will also pray a little for himself. And so I wrote on a note:

Please, Hashem,
Look down from Your Holy Residence and have mercy on Your People
Israel. Take your People Israel out of the Russian exile. Save my family,
please protect my Father and also take me out of here because it is very
hard for me.

And I had also learned that when the prophet Daniel did not know the direction of the Temple, he stood beside an open window and directed his heart to Jerusalem. The window in my prison cell was small, closed and barred. And could not be opened. But my heart was directed to the Temple Mount, to the city of Zion, to Jerusalem. My heart went out to Jerusalem.

A Jewish young man stands in a dark cell, leans against the wall, his head uplifted to the heavens. And it is as if there is no time. Suddenly, the warder bursts into the cell. 'What are you doing next to the wall? Trying to escape?' He searches in my pockets. He finds the note with the prayer. 'What is this? We shall take the note for translation.'

The next day the polite interrogator reads the translation and loses his temper. 'What, you are religious? You are not like us?'

I had won!

10. ORDERLY PRAYER

I was sentenced to twelve years' imprisonment and sent to a forced labour camp. There are Jews there, but no holy books. No Chumash, no Siddur, and I want to continue to pray. I no longer violate my decision to pray. But how? Shall I write a prayer again? But I do have a Passover Haggada which I managed to hide during the search, and in which there are passages of Tehillim, the Psalms of King David. I will learn them by heart and I will be able to pray all the time.

I must find a hiding place. I am in the corridor of the camp toilets. Dozens of people enter the toilets. I stand in the corridor,

A barrack in Camp No. 36 where I was held until my release in 1981.

facing the window, opposite the main entrance to the camp. When the patrol arrives I still have a little time to hide the Haggada and to get away. Is one permitted to recite and study holy words at the entrance to the toilets? I don't know. But what shall I do? I have to pray. I must...

Later on, I am in the plant. Friends inform me that they have managed to smuggle into the camp a Siddur and a Chumash. Unbelievable! When, at last, will I be able to hold them in my hands? In the evening they bring us back to our living quarters. There, those same friends had hidden the books among the work implements. My hands are shaking. Will I be able to guard the property? Will I be able to learn? Now I am really facing a test? All the time I said that I wanted to pray but I could not. And now I can.

It is so hard, so unpleasant, to pray in secret, clandestinely. I feel on my back the eyes of the gentile prisoners, the collaborators with the Nazis. Jew-haters. If they know they will inform. How will I conceal my praying? I will go to work on the night shift and then I will return at 6 a.m. At that time no one is in the hut.

Fence and watchtower in Camp No. 36 in the Perm region.

I sit in the hiding place, among the wooden beams, and copy the prayer onto pieces of paper. I put the papers into a matchbox which I place in an underground cache. If they confiscate one set, I will retrieve the rest. Furthermore, I prepare in an exercise book a 'legal' Siddur.

I am successful. I have a Siddur. I pray three times a day, like any Jew. Hashem worked a miracle for me. In the course of writing, under tremendous pressure, I learnt to remember the prayers by heart. Now nobody will be able to take it from me! Now I am a free man!

During the day, I pray the Mincha and Maariv afternoon and evening prayers at work. It is possible to hide. The problem is in the morning, when we get up early and there is a prisoner roll-call before going off to work. When to pray? I have no choice, before the general reveille. It is cold, almost darkness. A normal prisoner steals another moment to remain in the refuge of dreams, whereas I get up and go out to the snow path leading to the prisoners' toilets. The path runs between piles of snow the height of a man. I dig myself in one of the piles a recess to hide in. Now, even if they catch me, I can say that I was going to the toilet.

I stand and pray, and I don't feel the cold. The patrol arrives, an officer and two soldiers. 'What are you doing here?' I am silent. 'Not answering? Do a body search on him. Check all his clothing!' They didn't find anything on me, because the prayer is in the heart. They didn't find, but they felt. They knew I was doing something against them, against their will. And they were angry: 'We will catch you, and you will be punished. We know everything.'

In the end they caught me. In the court they again sentenced me to three years in a closely guarded prison. This is the 'worth' of a prayer.

11. LIFE IN PRAYER

On the way to that prison I tried to learn more verses. More and more, until they confiscated the Siddur. The way was hard, A journey of many days in the prison train, a prison on wheels. One morning we arrived: 'Get out!' and we were thrown into a transit cell. I collapse with exhaustion and fall asleep, and in my heart anxiety that I would not miss the time for reciting the morning Shema.

I rise with an effort, cast off the tiredness and the fogginess of the senses. Shake myself like a tank crewman from a burning tank. I must continue. I clean the neglected cell, so that it should be proper for prayer. First of all, to pray. This is already in my blood, Baruch Hashem (Thank G-d).

Vladimir Prison, where I was held for three years under the sentence of the court for observing the Shabbat in the camp.

And since then, in every cell among the gentiles, in every situation, without hiding, I pray. Because a Jew prays.

Once, during the Amida prayer, I felt that my cell-mate was threatening me. Perhaps he wanted to kill me, perhaps he had simply gone mad because of the heavy sentence he had received. I pray. Not moving, not afraid. This is the Halacha (religious law). I finished and only then did I turn to him: 'What happened to you?'

At the daily roll-call they opened the doors of all the cells When they opened mine, I ran away from it. They chased me along the corridor, beat me and placed me in solitary confinement, which is a place where a prisoner goes crazy for lack of activity. Everyone sits alone and can think at his ease about anything he pleases. But about what? He has already thought all his thoughts, and there is not much that is new in the prison, and he doesn't know what to do with himself. But I knew.

The sign of the morning comes at 5 a.m. when they lock to the wall all the miserable wooden planks called 'bed'. Soon they will bring water. There is no time to be lost.

Yesterday, I left from the portion they assigned me half a cup of water. I wash my hands and begin to pray. What a supreme grace that I remember the prayer by heart. What a precious gift is the very prayer itself. I sing it, pronounce every word with real physical pleasure and satisfaction. I do not recite the prayer. I live within it. The prayer is my refuge, which I have built over the years. I enter inside the prayer, and the world doesn't exist for me.

Thus the hours pass in prayer. I awake for a moment to the prison life. They are distributing bread. The bread is still warm. I take a break and inhale its good smell. And straight away return to my praying. I am already at Tachanun, the prayer of supplication! Oy vavoy. So quickly…

12. 'I THANK THEE FOR THOU HAST ANSWERED ME'

And in this life sequence from prayer to prayer, of life in prayer, there is still another aspect.

I am on a hunger strike, demanding that they return to me the holy books which they have confiscated from me. There is a big advantage to a hunger strike as against the routine life of a prisoner. One doesn't have to work. One does not need to hurry. I sit closed up.

I wrote a letter to my sister in Israel: 'I feel like Moshe Rabenu (Moses our Teacher) on Mount Sinai.' This a clear hint that I have not eaten for forty days already, like Moshe Rabenu. But this is not just a hint. In truth I feel that I am standing today on the summit of the mountain, receiving the Torah from Hashem, and fighting with all my might and all my blood for my holy books. What a privilege!

Now I have the time to contemplate the world of Hashem. I made a special discovery. There, outside, all the time they run. To arrange things, to progress. I suddenly understood that here I can simply sit and not run. Time stands still. And I feel myself above time, above nature. And the soul sees Hashem and prays a prayer without words. Just like an angel.

It once happened that on Yom Kippur there occurred a transfer of prisoners to another place. Chaos, running, body searches, rummaging through personal belongings, no respite. It was not fitting for Yom Kippur, but there was no escape. I felt depressed and angry that I had no rest on the Day of Judgement, or perhaps this was already the judgement itself?

When I thought how Eretz Israel would be, I said: there I shall pray with my soul at peace. Today, when I stand during the Yom Kippur prayer in the yeshiva hall in the silence of the Viduy confession prayer, there return and arise within me memories of the prison, pictures of the difficulty and suffering, like black scribblings on a beautiful and colourful picture. Now, from within the silence of prayer I know that I am in Israel.

Chapter 4

Passing Over

13. THE PASSOVER FESTIVAL/FATHER'S SEDER

I grew up in a world very far from the world of Judaism. It was a world entirely red: the Bolshevik Revolution, Lenin, Stalin, Communism. It is a wonder then how the Passover Seder night finds a place in the consciousness of a boy, built on these slogans.

I can't remember when Father began to hold the Passover Seder at home. Perhaps only when he was released from prison, and without Mother. I don't think that Father had any special problem about renewing the custom of the Passover Seder. He told me that our maternal grandfather used to invite him to participate in the Passover Seder in their house, even though, in those years before the Second World War, Father didn't observe the Mitzvot and was active in a Communist underground. It is interesting that Grandfather used to invite him. Perhaps by doing so he wished to plead the cause of his son-in-law and daughter, and it is interesting that Father accepted Grandfather's invitation. He didn't reject it even though he was an atheist and a communist. And perhaps he wasn't such an atheist, for otherwise how did he agree to hold a religious ceremony in the home of his father-in-law, a Chabad Hassid?

Perhaps some kind of answer lies in that Passover Seder which my father conducted anew. The very fact that the Seder was held according to the Haggada, even in the 1960s, was something special, even though there were certainly several thousand other Jews throughout Russia who kept the tradition. Because we didn't possess a Pesach Haggada, therefore Father conducted the Seder from memory, and his memory didn't betray him. Only later on did we come by a very fine Haggada, with illustrations and a Russian translation.

But that wasn't in my opinion the main thing. The uniqueness of my father's Seder resided in the story of the Exodus from Egypt. Father would begin from Adam, the First Man, and end with the history of the revival of the People of Israel in the modern era. This was still a great innovation to me.

Here at the Seder table we learned the history of the Jewish People, and also received a Zionist outlook. Consequently, the Pesach Seder performed its function wonderfully, as our Sages foresaw: 'And thou shall tell it to your son.' This wasn't just an empty saying. This was a Haggada that was a command, a transmission. Things that are said to the son, something of them will remain in him.

I can testify about myself that I grew up as a Jew thanks to the story of the Exodus from Egypt. This, if you will, is my 'Girsa Diynkuta', my knowledge acquired in childhood.

14. PESACH SHENI, THE SECOND PASSOVER

Pesach Sheni was meant for lepers, or for those who were on a distant road and unable to celebrate the Passover at the right time. We were all there, in the Soviet Union, like diseased persons, afflicted with all manner of mental diseases. Contaminated souls.

However, paradoxically, this time I mean something else. It was a Passover Seder which I conducted in the 1960s as an aliya activist on behalf of the underground Zionist organization. I was informed that the organization had located a group of Jewish youth who were not opposed to holding a Passover Seder in a private home. Obviously, in those days this was an undesirable thing. Participation in a national religious ceremony was liable to disqualify the participants from a good career for life. Apparently, they were not sufficiently adult to make this calculation, and so they responded positively to my proposal.

It was a typical house of a Jewish family in Riga, and that day was not a Passover night but one of the intermediate days of the festival, which began as a regular day. The house was full of Chametz (leavened bread and food) and the group made up of distinctly Jewish types. For such as these we endangered our lives later on.

I brought with me a fine, illustrated Passover Haggada, also Matzot for the dish, a little bit of luxury in those days. The mother of the household, a 'Yiddishe Mama', made gefilte fish (fish balls) for us. I began to conduct the Seder with a monotonous tone of reciting, accompanied by my cumbersome translation. I did not have enough experience and I didn't know how I would introduce in the Seder

News conference in the United Nations, New York, 1981. I show a tallit which I made illegally in the prison. Next to me is the Israeli UN Ambassador, Yehuda Blum.

experience that part which I had learned from Father. If only I had known how! But I was zealous for the word of Hashem and I read word for word. I am surely boring the group, I thought. I saw the young men and girls getting up from the table and beginning to dance. Just imagine my feelings. Had I not come on such an important mission, to save my people from the Galut, and here they were dancing! I got up and left in anger.

Several days later, I met in the street one of the young men from that group. He came over to me and said: 'What a pity that you left then so suddenly. It was very interesting all what you told us. We spoke until late at night how to emigrate to Israel. Perhaps you know how?' Then I already knew the way, but I didn't tell him. I knew that the way is, according to the words of the Haggada, 'with a strong hand'. I couldn't tell him.

Once, after I was expelled from prison to Israel, I was walking in King George Street in Jerusalem and an unknown woman approached me and said: 'Do you remember the Seder which you held for us in Riga? I too was there, and thanks to you we emigrated to Israel! I have been here already for ten years!'

Thanks to the Passover Seder we had been redeemed from Russia.

15. WITH A MIGHTY HAND

The connection between the attempted hijacking and Passover was as follows. After I had succeeded in 'changing my judgement', as King David puts it, before the recruitment commission of the Russian army, I went directly to the Ministry of the Interior and showed the official my (deficient fitness) certificate. 'You see you have no reason to hold me, because I am of no value.' The official was angry and said to me, just like Pharaoh: 'Go away from here and forget about your Israel. You will work here and build our Communism for us. Here we shall bury you. We shall not send you to serve in an army that is fighting against our Arab friends.'

I also thought according to the words of the Haggada: 'And the Lord took us out from there with a mighty hand and an outstretched arm.' But how would we come by this 'mighty hand'? And then, with great mercy, Hashem wrought the miracle.

One of the loyal bodyguards of the Soviet ruler in his palace was a Jewish major named Mark Dimshitz, who had served in a combat flight squadron on the Afghan border. When Hashem sought to take his people out of the land of exile, He asked the angels – so I believe – 'who shall we send?' The angels answered: 'Him we shall send,' and pointed to the major in the Russian air force. Immediately the Holy One Blessed Be He planted in his head the thought that he was a Jew, and that he had a Jewish state with a Jewish army, and that he must save it from its enemies. And since the thought was implanted, his sleep wandered and he knew no rest. They expelled him from the army.

He came to the big city and went to look for a book with the holy letters. As he was sitting thus in the National Library and studying the Hebrew letters, a Jew who knew the form of the Hebrew letters approached him and asked him: 'Why are you looking at that?' Mark Dimshitz thought that he was an informer, but he was not afraid. He said to himself 'Here is the test which I have to pass, and not to betray my people.' He said to him: 'I am a Jew, and I came to learn the Holy Tongue which you gentiles have stolen from me.' The man answered him: 'I am also a Jew, don't be suspicious of me. I will take you to a place of refuge and teach you the Holy Tongue.' Thus thanks to the Holy Tongue and his courage when he said 'I am a Jew', the salvation began to burst forth.

The Jewish officer came to the hiding place where the young men of Israel were learning the Holy Tongue, and he saw young Jewish men sitting and learning. He at once asked himself in amazement: 'Are there other Jews loyal to the people of Israel like me?' And one should know that when he served in the ruler's palace he thought that he was the only Jew in that place who pledged loyalty to the Jewish people. He told them: 'If you are many and want to go to Eretz Israel, I shall take you.' And he took them.

Immediately the news spread among the faithful. A way had been found to leave the land of exile, the northern land, to Eretz Israel. Hundreds of Jews gathered . But it was a hard road, which required of them personal responsibility and great courage. In the end we remained just a quorum of Jews.

At that time the Holy One Blessed Be He whispered into the ears of the wicked ones: 'Faithful sons have banded together to immigrate to Eretz Israel.' The gentiles jumped with glee: 'We shall set a trap for them, and they will cause their people to fall into the trap, and they will stink in the eyes of the world.' And so it was.

We came, the ten of us Jews, to the airfield, to try to flee on eagles' wings to Eretz Israel. But the Russians caught all of us. The wicked ones began to celebrate over the fresh Jewish blood they scented. They did not only catch us, but they also made it public: 'You see, these

Jews are not loyal to our state! They want to flee! Their judgement will be one, to kill, to destroy, and to perish.'

And the Children of Israel cried out, and Hashem heard. And a Shechina (Divine radiance) descended and covered the pit of the prison into which the Prisoners of Zion had been thrown. And Hashem hardened the heart of the Russians to put the Prisoners of Zion on trial, so that all the Jews should learn what shall be done to a Jew that is not loyal to the Soviet State.

And the people of Israel in every place where they resided declared a day of outcry and despair, and Jews came in their thousands and hundreds of thousands to the palaces of the gentiles to cry out and demand the rescue of their brethren.

Then Hashem opened the hearts of the rulers of the gentiles in all the states, and they began to send to the rulers of Russia letters and notes to shame them for wanting to perpetrate such an injustice.

And the ruler of the Russians named 'the possessor of the eyebrows' (Leonid Brezhnev, the Secretary of the Communist Party) asked: 'Who is he and which is he who has hatched this plot and caused our state to fall into the trap?' Immediately, they found the guilty one and stripped him of all his ranks, he and all his aides with him. And the Children of Israel came out with an upraised hand. Thus did I see with my own eyes the hand of Hashem and the parting of the Red Sea.

16. 'AND JOSEPH WAS TAKEN DOWN TO EGYPT'

The name of Amalek was not erased, and his seed still rules in the land.

After the trial which was held for us, the ten partners of 'Operation Wedding', the slander began to emerge from the jaw of the crocodile. Many Jews began to emigrate to Israel. We remained imprisoned, swallowed up like a foreign body in the jaw of the predator, almost to the point of choking.

And yet, this too, Hashem meant for the best, because many of the exiles sank in the waters of their insignificance, they were not called by their name nor did they guard their tongue. In order to arouse them and to grasp them by the tuft of their heads and to shake them, the Prisoners of Zion would have had to defend them from within the exile, like a bleeding wound harming the whole body, and to plead the cause of the weaker ones.

For many years we were waiting for when the choking would lead to release, and when the bleeding wound would heal.

My name is Joseph and I am in the Diaspora. For eleven years I was at the bottom of the pit. 11 like the number 'Eretz Israel' (initial letters Alef Yud=11) to teach you that Eretz Israel was bought by Yud Alef, and that I spent 11 Passovers in prison. Eleven times the danger passed over me, until I had completed my mission in the exile, to join the sparks and to make amends, and I passed overnight from the land of exile to the Holy Land. Each Pesach in prison a great repair took place. I wish to tell about two of them.

In 1977 a parcel of a kilogram of Matzot (unleavened flatbread) was sent to me, which was according to the prison regulation which permitted one to receive a kilo of baked items from home. The parcel arrived, but they didn't give it to me. All my requests were in vain. The answer was: 'If you deserve it you will get it one of these days.' I understood that they wanted to maltreat me and to delay the delivery of the parcel until after the festival. How can we be without Matza on Pesach? And were not all the other Jewish prisoners, three in number, dependent on my Matza?

Hashem brought the prison commandant round to me. One day, I was working manually in the forced labour installation, and I felt that someone was standing near and watching me. I turned around – the commandant! Lieutenant-Colonel Mikof! Whilst still engaged in the work effort I ran to him to talk about the non-delivery of the Matzot. I spoke to him emphatically, that if they didn't give me the Matzot now I would make trouble for them. The Lieutenant Colonel recoiled from me and said: 'Very well, I will see to it already.' And while speaking he moved backwards until he disappeared from view.

When Mikof disappeared, another prisoner approached me. 'What did you do, are you mad?'

'What have I done then? I simply spoke to him.'

'Simply? Weren't you holding a hammer in your hand when you spoke with the Lieutenant-Colonel, and this is considered an attempt to attack an officer on duty in aggravated circumstances. You will be punished for it.'

He predicted, and he was right. On that selfsame day I was summoned to the headquarters, and the packet of Matzot was handed to me. I opened it and saw that all the Matzot were broken into fragments. 'Why did you break them?' I asked, boiling with anger. But the miracle happened. I had received Matzot and it was on 14 Nissan.

'We suspected that there was a letter in the parcel and it was all written in code. Every biscuit was marked with dots, as if they had written words on it.'

They wanted to spoil the letter sent to us from Hashem, and they didn't succeed. I held a Passover Seder for my friends according to the law, except that there was no wine and we drank water.

On the day after the festival, the 'Isru Chag', I was summoned to the headquarters and led to the court where they sentenced me to three years imprisonment under severest conditions 'for observing the Commandments and for behavior threatening the peace of the camp'. This was the revenge of Lieutenant-Colonel Mikof. Thanks to my fight for the Matzot, I was sent to the bottom of the pit.

In Kabbalistic Gematria the Hebrew initial letters of the Soviet Union, רסס, have the equivalent numerical value of Mitzrayim (מירצמ) – Egypt.

17. THE HAGGADA OF YOSEF

One cannot compare a Seder in the forced labour camp with one in a closed prison. Here there is no place to hide from the sight of the gentiles imprisoned with me in a narrow cell. Six people sit together and each one sees what is happening in the plate of the other one.

On the first Passover in the prison, I turned to my non-Jewish companions and explained to them that on Passover I did not eat or have in my possession any Chametz. I had a small shelf inside a little cupboard in which I kept foodstuffs for all the prisoners in the cell. I washed it down with water and covered it with a piece of newspaper. I told them that I was keeping the place for myself alone and that they shouldn't put bread there. And I also arranged with them that I would forego my daily portion of bread, and that they could take it and do what they wished with it. Since I was forbidden to enjoy the Chametz, I warned them against wanting to give me any other food in its place. Such an exchange was also considered as selling bread and was forbidden.

To the credit of those prisoners, I must say that they understood the religious practice, and when on Passover they would offer me a piece of potato or herring, they stressed that it was a gift and not instead of the bread.

On the evening of the search for leavened bread, Bedikat Hametz, I undertook a search. I crawled under the bunks with a lit match in hand, instead of a candle. The prisoners, as usual, sat on the two-tiered bunks and gazed down on me from above. What I was doing must have seemed very pathetic. 'What, are you looking for bread? Don't worry we gobbled-up everything in the morning,' they laughed.

And not from hatred. They were freedom fighters, opponents of the regime, our friends.

Thus did I sit in the centre of the cell and when I lifted my improvised dish and recited: 'Ho lachmo anyo di achlu avoteynu b'eretz Mitzrayim' (This is the bread of affliction that our ancestors ate in the land of Egypt), the Matzot were not in the eyes of everyone the bread of affliction at all but white biscuits, pleasant to the sight. Since I realized what was happening in the stomachs of my fellow cellmates, I distributed to them also small pieces from the Matza, and they ate with great pleasure, without fearing that there was Christian blood in them.

On my third Passover in prison I was in a small cell with one Jew and a gentile. I suggested to the Jew, named Gili, that we should hold a proper Pesach. He only laughed: 'You must be dreaming. A kosher Seder in prison – impossible.' Since I was aware of his skeptical nature, I did not go on arguing, but I started to make preparations for the festival.

All the circumstances were certainly interwoven with small miracles. First of all, I had with me a postcard from Israel on which there appeared an item from the Israel Museum – a Pesach dish from the seventeenth century in Germany. Thus I was able to easily recall the products required for Pesach such as Karpas, Maror, Haroset (parsley, bitter herbs, fruit and nut paste) and others and, what was more important still, someone, in his wisdom, had written on the side of the postcard all the sections of the Seder. I sat down to write the content of the Seder night according to what was in the list. Here I was assisted by my experience of conducting a Seder which I had gained still from my days in the underground in Riga. After I had prepared the spiritual part, I began to deal with the foodstuffs.

First of all, wine. I had a small packet of raisins which my father Moshe, of Blessed Memory, had given me when I was still under interrogation. I had looked after the raisins well for over ten years, and had used only two raisins on Shabbat. This time I decided to make real wine from them. I hoarded sugar for the whole month. Every day they would allocate 15 grams of sugar to each prisoner. Each one of the prisoners certainly did not lose the opportunity to drink warm water with sugar, to sip each sip separately, while shutting his eyes with pleasure. Had I been imprisoned with real criminals they would immediately have stolen the sugar from me, but the political prisoners only looked at me in amazement. I added the sugar to the raisins and mixed the whole with water inside a water bottle which I hid among rags beneath my prison bunk. All that I needed was for them to discover

the water bottle during a routine search. Not only is he a terrorist and
a religious fanatic, but he is also an alcoholic! And here a miracle
occurred, and for those seven days during which I prepared the wine,
until the eve of the festival, no scarches took place at all!

The prisoners were even more amazed when they distributed
among the prisoners little onions. There was a flu epidemic, and the
humane authorities did not find a better means of preventing an
outbreak of the disease than the distribution of a small onion to each
prisoner. Everyone fell on this gift as if it had fallen on us from Heaven.
Raw fruit! Sweet as candy...No one paid attention to the tears which
streamed from their eyes whilst they ate it. As for me, I noticed that
this might serve me for Chrein (horseradish and beet), even though one
could cry in prison without Chrein, but one could not, Heaven forbid,
compare an onion tear with one from misfortune. In order for my
onion not to go bad I put it in a jar of water and would gain more profit
from it if it would produce leaves which I would also be able to use as
Karpas. The prisoners laughed – Yosef the gardener! One must really
be crazy to grow decorative greenery at a time of hunger. I remained
silent.

However, Hashem ordered a different type of greenery for Karpas
for me. They would take us out every day for an hour to walk in the
yard. These were small roofless rooms divided by cement walls so that
a prisoner from one cell could not heaven forbid see a prisoner from
another cell.

This was an opportunity to see Hashem's heavens and to breathe
the air, because these rooms were built on the roof very close to the
heavens. And so, as I went out from such a yard, I noticed that in the
adjacent yard, under the asphalt, there grew a single blade of grass.
Since I had become in the labour camp an expert on eating herbs, I
immediately identified it as an edible herb. I prayed in my heart that
they would not pick it before the time, and on the eve of the festival
I ran to that place, and as the warder shouted at me with all his might
I picked the herb. It was big and very suitable to be Karpas. I told
the warder that this was a medicinal herb, and he was so interested
in the healing properties of medicinal herbs that he even forgot to
punish me.

Thus, by the eve of the festival, I was ready for the Seder. I also
found a solution for the egg and the Zeroa (lamb shankbone). I had kept
some spoonfuls of egg powder which my sisters had sent me from Israel
and which I shaped like an egg. For the Zeroa I had an Osem soup cube
which was also one of the prisoner's closely-guarded treasures.

Out of paper cut from the *Pravda* newspaper I fashioned a bowl and on it I wrote the names of the symbols: Hazeret, Zeroa, Karpas etc. The Haggada, which I wrote from memory, was ready, and then I invited Gili and, of course, also the gentile to the Passover Seder. Gili burst out laughing: 'Are you still talking that nonsense. Didn't I tell you that it was impossible to hold a Passover Seder under the conditions we have here?'

I uncovered the bowl for him, and was happy that it held in it all that was required. He checked every single thing, and finally asserted: 'But you don't have the four cups! I told you!' I brought out from beneath the bunk the water bottle. He pulled out the cork with a suspicious look, smelled, and began to smile. Real wine! The smile and the smell broke the resistance, and we sat down for the 'Seder' on the bed. We prayed that the warders would not break in and disturb us. When I finished everything, including the songs I had learned from my father, Gili said to me:'For the first time in my life I have attended a proper Passover Seder.' And I thought that this was perhaps symbolic of the generation, that the Jew comes to hold his first Passover Seder precisely in jail.

The next day, first thing in the morning, Gili was called to pack his belongings and to leave the cell. He was taken from the prison to an unknown destination. But my heart told me that he had been released and had gone to Eretz Israel. And so it was. Not only Gili but most of my friends were suddenly taken out following a prolonged struggle by Jews in the free world.

Even though I did not know what exactly had happened to Gili, the assumption that he had been released added a fresh dimension to my feeling of Passover. It was a feeling of spring, which wells up and grows together with the exciting sense of something great and joyful. Thus, I suppose, did the Children of Israel feel on leaving Egypt. Still not freedom, but already the scent of freedom. Thus did this Seder night become, and perhaps thanks to the Seder, a real Passover.

Chapter 5

Shabbat

18. THE REDEEMING SHABBAT

Although I had decided even before my arrest to observe the Sabbath, I was not too successful, and I also didn't know how to keep it. When I began my struggle against the interrogator and against my weakness and decided to remain a Jew, it was clear to me that I must keep the Shabbat.

The solitary confinement cell in Chistopol Prison, 1980.

How to keep the Shabbat inside a cell in the interrogation facility of the KGB? Not to put on the light? How shall we put it on, since, in any case, isn't the switch in the hands of the warders? On weekdays, when we went to sleep, the light above our heads shone continuously. We were compelled to sleep with our faces upwards and our hands on our chest so that, in the dark, under the blanket, we could not cut our veins. The KGB authorities knew that we had enough reasons to commit such an act. If only it had been possible to put out the blinding light.

At any rate, I found a way to mark the Shabbat with a Hechsher Mitzvah (preparation for a Mitzvah). I asked the warder for a rag to wash the floor and the walls. The place was really very dirty. Once I complained to my 'intelligent' interrogator about the difficult conditions prevailing in the cell, and he found a reason for justifying this: 'We didn't build the prison facility. The Nazis built a prison here for the Gestapo during the war.' More than once I imagined an anonymous Jew sitting here after being caught by the Nazis, may their name be blotted out.

Nonetheless, the difficult atmosphere of the cell, the figures of my predecessors who populated the place, and also the heavy foreboding about the future, failed to sway me from my decision to observe the Sabbath. Furthermore, the Shabbat was a place of refuge, inside which I could feel more secure and cut off from the hostile environment. Therefore, every item and every thing that I managed to accumulate for the sake of the day were the basic bricks with which I built the wall.

I had a white shirt which relatives had given me, a sort of vest which served me uniquely as a Shabbat garment. After Shabbat I would launder it under the tap.

And thus did I celebrate the Shabbat: I found a nail and cut two grooves in the wall to represent the Shabbat candles. I remembered the formula for *Licht Benchen*, for blessing the candles, although I had never ever seen it.

And those raisins, that whole kilo of raisins which my father of blessed memory had given me when I was arrested and which I had kept for almost eleven years of imprisonment, (and had to keep because, when they transferred me to a camp, it was forbidden to receive raisins), they served me as a substitute for wine. In the underground I had learnt the blessing over wine, 'Borei Pri Hagefen' (Creator of the fruit of the vine), and wished to add it to my Shabbat treasures. Since the raisins were the fruit of the vine, so I thought, it was permitted to bless over them, and so mistakenly I acted. But then it was a mistake of a Mitzvah, because thereby I observed the Mitzvah of remembering the Shabbat.

The warders kept track of my unusual practices as a prisoner, and all of this was entered into my criminal file as proof that I was a big criminal deserving of a severe punishment. The interrogators gather proof against the detainee during the investigation in all kinds of ways: phone tapping, planting provocateurs in the cell, etc. They did this also to me until they described me at my trial as 'a religious fanatic', and ever since then nobody has bestowed a more honorable title on me.

19. CELEBRATING THE SHABBAT

It was a real act of labour. Especially when they took me after the trial to a forced labour camp where we were like the slaves of the Russian Pharaoh who oppressed us under the slogan 'work reforms'.

After a period of interrogation and trial I finally came to the camp itself. I went out to its spacious courtyard and breathed the air and gazed at the skies. I discovered life anew. I was full of wonder at everything I saw in nature. There was even one small tree there. I sat down beside it and stroked its leaves. 'Hello, tree. And even if you are a tree of exile, I love you. I could have been killed and I have remained alive. Thank you, Hashem.'

I scarcely had time to enjoy all this abundance, because prisoners came and said: 'There is one prisoner, named Grilius. He is just now in the factory department. He heard that you have come and asks you to approach the fence because he has to speak to you urgently.' What did I care about some Latvian or Lithuanian gentile (that is how his names sounded)? But they told me over and over again. I relented, and went to see what he wanted from me. I went close to the fence, as close as I could, and could not get any closer because of the security area which contained five rows of sharp barbed wire and wooden fencing. I saw from a distance a man of medium height with a red beard. He raised a hand and shouted to me: 'Hello, friend. How are you?' He spoke in the Holy Tongue. I was amazed. Here, in the camp, I meet a Jew speaking Hebrew. My heart beat fast with joy. And I waited for his arrival at the living quarters section.

When he came, we embraced like brothers. It turned out that he had already been two years in prison. He and his friends, the brothers Arie and Zeev Vadka, had decided after their trial to observe the Mitzvot. 'How does one observe the Mitzvot?' was the first question which Grilius asked me. 'When I heard that they had arrested Jews who had tried to escape to Eretz Israel, I prayed that they would send me one who knew to speak Hebrew and knew Torah. Now I ask you: Do you know this? Can you teach me?'

It was a difficult test. Had his prayers been answered by my arrival? After all, I was the only one among all the prisoners who somehow knew how to meet his demands. Therefore, I had been sent to him. I told him once that he had the merit of the forefathers.'Then, if you know what it means to be a Jew, teach me at once, because I am incapable of remaining, and not for a moment more, in my gentile state!'

I unfolded before him all my Torah on one leg. Shabbat, kashrut, prayer and covering the head. It is easier in the camp than in the prison. There is here a needle and thread. From the wide prisoner's uniform we cut strips of material, and from them I sewed kippot. We also managed with the dietary laws of Kashrut.

Shimon, for that was the name of the veteran prisoner, found a way to manage to keep the Shabbat. The prisoners had to hand over at the end of the day their quota of work to the prisoner in charge. Therefore, we would try to prepare an extra portion of work during the week and hand it over to the man in charge before Shabbat. On Shabbat we would go out together with all the prisoners, to the plant, but would avoid working. It was not easy to all the time evade the sight of the inspectors and to give the impression that we were working. And I didn't want to keep the Shabbat demonstratively because the Shabbat was not intended for demonstrations. It was a sign between me and Hashem.

When more Jews joined, we decided to hold a Kabbalat Shabbat to welcome the Sabbath. Once again, we had no idea of the Halacha. Nonetheless we would light candles. I distributed two raisins to each person, and after that we would eat something tasty which Shimon would prepare for us.

Every gathering of prisoners was forbidden, and especially for a religious ceremony. Therefore, each time we would search for a place, an abandoned hut or 'Kaptiorka', a place for drying clothes, in order to meet together for a short time until a police patrol appeared. One of us stood guard outside and gave a sign: 'Hevra, guys, disperse!' Oy vey, how I understand the Marrano Jews in Spain!

20. 'AND ON THE SABBATH DAY, TWO HE-LAMBS OF THE FIRST YEAR WITHOUT BLEMISH'

Seven years had passed. Although the warders disturbed, we could manage. Shimon left and immigrated to Eretz Israel. Other friends left.

After their release the situation changed. The gentiles began to pester and persecute.

One Shabbat I went out to the plant. I immediately found a quiet spot, from which one could keep an eye on the camp gate and retreat into the plant when the patrol arrived. I hid myself behind a pile of stinking prisoners' clothes, and began to pray the Shaharit morning prayer of Shabbat from slips of paper which I drew out from the concealed match box. I don't know how, but the warders entered without my seeing them, and caught me 'in the act'. The police blocked my path of retreat to the plant area. The group was headed by the notorious sadist, Major Fedorov. His eyes were red and his nose almost shook with the joy of a hunting dog. 'Mendelevich, why aren't you in the work place?'

As usual I mumbled something and went in the direction of the work installations. But this time it was clear to me that they had come to catch me. They were also not going to let me simply retreat, but would accompany me to the plant and see me desecrate the Sabbath in their presence.

I did not know many Halachot. But once I read something that had become impressed clearly on my memory, namely that: If the gentile forces me to desecrate one of the statutes of the Torah in order to harm the Jewish people and Hashem – G-d forbid! – one must die rather than desecrate. I confessed to Hashem that I was left with no choice.

'I don't work on the Sabbath because Jews are forbidden to work on the Sabbath.'

'Go immediately to the work place. Apparently, you have forgotten where you are. You will rot in solitary confinement and you will never see your Israel in your lifetime.'

'I'm not afraid of you. Hashem alone do I fear.'

'Take him at once to solitary confinement!'

Two policemen escorted me. It was the month of March. The snow was deep. I walked in the snow escorted by the warders, and I was happy, and in my heart I thanked Hashem for having given me the merit of such a big Mitzvah of self-sacrifice for the sake of the Shabbat.

I said in my heart: 'There are those who receive punishment from Heaven for not keeping Shabbat. But is there anyone else who receives punishment for observing the Shabbat?' .....They brought me to the solitary confinement, and the sentence was a month's sitting in a particularly harsh punishment cell known as P.K.T. with minimum food or sleep. There was nothing special about this punishment. I had endured it before. I planned how I would get out of here and hold a Passover Seder among my friends. I decided to continue acting as always, and to keep the work quota also for the Sabbath. (Even during the solitary confinement we were not exempted from working.) I intended this so as not to give a reason to punish me whilst I was sitting in solitary.

My manoeuvre to be able to provide the work quota for the Shabbat was very simple. What type of work could they invent for people sitting in a dark cellar? They found some. To make screwing threads in spare parts of cars. It was done by hand, and the work quota was very low. Therefore, it was not a problem on weekdays to prepare a 'spare' for Shabbat. But where to keep it? Here, too, I was able to find a 'patent'. They had built the solitary in a very primitive way from tree trunks. The floor was also made from wooden planks. Perhaps because of this, in winter it was colder, but it helped me very much. I checked and found that between the planks there were slits, and under the planks big hollows. Therefore, I would string all the parts on a string I had managed to steal, and lower them down beneath the floor. As soon as Shabbat was out, I would deliver the work.

I checked that the warder was not watching me and I bent over and pulled the string. I pulled slowly because the string was liable to break. And suddenly the string broke! All my toil went down the drain. But not to worry. Like a practical Jew, I had prepared for myself several caches. In the end I managed and pulled up the parts.

Thus, a month passed, and I came back to the camp before Passover as I had planned. I regarded this enterprise as a big achievement. On the one hand, as far as possible I had not endangered myself, and, on the other hand, I had kept the Shabbat and the Pesach despite all the dangers.

On Isru Chag they ordered me to pack my belongings. This was a sign of moving to another camp. They transported me in a prisoner's car that was completely sealed. I breathed in the gases being emitted from the engine. The car travelled willy-nilly through the forest. I felt terrible. In general, I am very sensitive to traveling. Even on a bus I would vomit. I told myself that I wouldn't humiliate myself before them and wouldn't look miserable in their sight. I would do everything not to vomit, and would not beg for mercy. I shut my eyes. I told myself: 'I am a son of Hashem. He loves me. I am risking my life for the Shabbat. Hashem will surely protect me.' And then I felt myself as if I were a baby whose warm and loving father was rocking me. They were not the jolts of the journey. I prayed to Hashem and asked Him to protect me. I won! I left the car quietly and confidently.

They brought me to the court in the city, and a camp representative read the accusation:

'Mendelevich is living the life of a parasite. Refuses to work. Has a bad influence on other prisoners. Violates the camp regulations. Stops the prisoners from mending their ways.' These were harsh accusations. One could get the impression that I was a very hardened criminal. 'Has a bad influence on his comrades', meaning he draws them close to Torah and Mitzvot. Nonetheless, I was accorded the right of response: 'I do not refuse to work. Just on Shabbat I do not work, for religious reasons.'

I was very surprised when the Judge, this time it was a woman judge, examined the dates of the reports they laid on her desk, reports which reviewed my refusals to work. She was convinced of the justice of my claims, and turned to the deputy camp commandant who had submitted the charge sheet. 'He is right. Why didn't you give me a true report?'

I don't know what they did to the brave woman judge. A state prosecutor demanded that they make a break in the hearing. Apparently, they explained to this good woman who she was defending. After the break, she declared with cast-down eyes the sentence: three years imprisonment under the severest conditions.

Never mind, I said to myself. Shabbat is worth more. In fact, I was happy that I had received the punishment. It meant that I would continue to struggle for my people.

Am Israel Chai! (The People of Israel live!)

21. IN AN HOTEL ON THE WAY TO THE PIT

Although, from the point of view of the wicked ones, this was a very harsh punishment, nevertheless, a prisoner sentenced to a labour camp is in an open territory, even though he is fenced in and guarded. I can see the sky and the sun. There are hundreds of people. We can meet and talk. Almost real living, despite all the limitations. In prison, on the other hand, one sits all the time in a cell, apart from a short 'stroll' in a roofless cell. Scant food, stench, no air to breathe. Tension. Such conditions are life-shortening. At the same time, many decent people chose voluntarily not to be enslaved to an extra slice of bread. To be free people.

On the way to Vladimir Prison, which was notorious as a place of punishment for hundreds of years, I was privileged to spend time in an 'hotel', although one without stars. Instead of sending me directly to Vladimir they transferred me to the adjacent camp, No. 35, and placed me in solitary confinement. This was surely an overt miracle. I sat for several weeks quietly. No inspectors. No need to work. I sat in a big cell and studied Torah. This was an additional overt miracle.

Several years previously, my companions had managed to bribe one warder and to smuggle a Siddur and Tanach into the camp. I would study the Tanach in the 'Red Corner', a room in a hut designated for reading Communist literature. Thus I would sit and learn. As a rule they didn't make searches in the 'Red Corner'. One day I was reading the Book of Job, Chapter 7. Suddenly, a soldier from the Ministry of the Interior entered. I understood that they were conducting a general search in the camp. An entire unit of soldiers had entered the camp so that there was no time to move or to hide anything.

I might lose the Tanach! I must act! Feeling that all was lost, I ran to the place for drying clothes. There they were drying the prisoners' clothing, because at the end of the work day everything was wet from the snow. I went inside. The soldiers had not yet reached here. I hid the book inside the sleeve of my work garment and went out. At the entrance there stood a soldier smiling. He understood everything. They found the book and confiscated it as 'anti-Soviet propaganda'. Nothing helped, despite a hunger strike and complaints to the state attorney.

But now, on the way to the prison, I received the Tanach back. According to the prison regulations, every item that was confiscated was returned to the prisoner until he reached a new place of imprisonment. A strange clause, but one must give the Russians credit for acting upon it.

And they also returned to me a Tallit Katan (a small prayer shawl). It was the gift of my friend, Shimon Grilius, after he had completed the five years of imprisonment he had been sentenced to. Before his release I had asked him to send me a Tallit Katan. I had never seen a Tallit Katan, but I knew that one must wear it, and Shimon, as always, kept his promise. One day they called me to the command headquarters. 'A parcel has arrived for you from Grilius.' My heart beat rapidly within me with joy. Finally I would wrap myself in a Tallit!

But they didn't hand it over to me yet. They only showed it from a distance. What is this strange thing? I understand what is being referred to, but I look for a way to explain: 'It does indeed look strange. It is a vest which is a part of our national costume…' I try to be evasive, and they laugh- 'We know what Grilius can send you. A religious item! It does not appear on the list of prisoner clothing. The item is confiscated.'

And now, behold, after the trial, I am sitting in my 'hotel' wrapped in a Tallit and studying Torah. I made a special effort to learn Tehillim by heart, especially the hymn 'Yoshev Beseter Elyon' (He who dwells in the shelter of the Most High). But to every good thing comes an end. One morning they loaded me once again onto the prisoner train and sent me to Vladimir. I tried to activate my brain as I sat in my cell. How to save the treasure from renewed confiscation?

First of all, I solved the matter of the book. It occurred to me that I had a book in Yiddish, a language permitted for reading by prisoners. It was a collection of speeches of the head of the Communist Party, the dictator Leonid Brezhnev. If one could manage somehow to insert the Tanach inside the Yiddish book, this could be a successful solution. I took out this funny Yiddish book and suddenly noticed that its design was exactly like that of the Tanach, notwithstanding the world of difference between them, I immediately tore the cover of the book on which was also printed in Russian 'The Book has been approved by the State Publishing Company'. I chewed a bit of bread until it became glue, and stuck the cover into the Tanach. Now I possessed a Tanach with a Soviet 'Hechsher' (certification), perhaps the first in all the days of the cruel regime. (However, I regretted that on Passover I would not be able to use the Tanach because of the Chametz in the glue.)

The second mission concerned the Tallit Katan. I also knew that the Tzitziot fringes were the main thing. Therefore, I removed them, and I threaded them one by one onto a pair of woollen socks, because it was permitted to possess two pairs. Now it looked as if a 'Pompom' had been added to the socks. And, in fact, the experiment was successful. In the search room of the prison they looked for money, ammunition and drugs. The book examination was perfunctory. The inspector cast a glance at the book cover with the 'Hechsher', and handed it back to me, while he shook out the pages of the book in case there was money concealed there (my money was sewn at the back of my slippers, but I was least of all concerned about it).

They brought me to a grayish and cold cell with a broken window. It was not so important. A person can get used to everything. I sat down on the mattress and opened the Book of Job, Chapter 7, in order to continue from where I had been rudely interrupted. That same day I also found a solution for the Tzitziot. I simply attached them to four corners of a woollen scarf and I wrapped myself in the scarf – a strictly kosher Mitzvah Tzitzit. In the end they informed me that the prisoners would not go out any longer to the plant and would remain permanently inside the cell. This meant that there would not be problems with observing the Shabbat.

Thus I found myself honoring the Mitzvot. And where? In the Soviet Gehinnom. Had they not thrown me into here as punishment for observing the Mitzvot? But Hashem thought otherwise, and thanks to my Mesirut Hanefesh for observing the Shabbat I had merited the Mitzvah of studying Torah and Mitzvat Tzitzit. As it is said: 'One Mitzvah draws another Mitzvah in its wake.' Precisely!

Since then I spent many Sabbaths in prison. I prepared for them the whole week, according to the words of Bet Shammai. Every good thing that came to me I left for Shabbat. Once, Natan Sharansky, who was in the next cell to mine, said to me:

'What happened, Yosef? You are very sick.'

'Why do you say that?'

'Because I listened, and I heard how many medicines you asked for.'

I laughed (the conversation was carried on via the toilet bowl which was connected to the same waste pipe).

'I am not sick, but am preparing for Shabbat.'

I asked for a herbal infusion for relief in order to drink a toast 'Lechaim' (to life), because the infusions were soaked in alcohol. I asked for mustard stickers because I would scrape the mustard from them, mix it with bread and make 'Forschmak' (pie). I would also collect portions of a small herring fish called Kilka, remove the bones and make a kind of 'Gefilte Fish' (fish balls), and also hoard bread so that on Shabbat at least I would be sated. But one Shabbat I remember in particular:

22. SHABBAT IN SOLITARY CONFINEMENT

I was given a punishment, fifteen days in solitary confinement. Like an experienced prisoner, I had organized in advance for the duration of the sentence. I took with me a handkerchief. When I was already in the solitary, a cold and narrow cellar, I divided the handkerchief into two parts: one for a kippa and the second as a cover for the Challot loaves on Shabbat. I have already told about prayer in the solitary.

In general, I took pains to collect all the delicacies as usual. The difficulty was that one day they did not give anything apart from a piece of bread. But the next day they gave herring. I saved the bread in honour of the Shabbat despite the hunger. The hardest part of the bread is the sweetest, and I would cut it with a makeshift knife made of a piece of wood. I found a hiding place between the cracks in one of the walls. Prisoners were forbidden to keep bread in the cell, in case it might serve them afterwards in their escape preparations. Therefore, I needed many hiding places.

In addition to keeping bread for Shabbat, I decided to keep a whole portion of bread and bring it out of the solitary into my cell. The food restriction is designed to turn the prisoner into a slave dependent on the good graces of the warders, and as one aspiring for freedom I could not be reconciled to this arbitrary restriction. Since I was unable to add to the size of the portion, I decided, as an expression of my free will and my personal freedom, to restrict myself in the amount of bread which I ate, and so I did.

The eve of Shabbat arrived. When one sits in a closed cell, one cannot distinguish between the times of the day because the window is not only double-barred but also closed with a perforated metal sheet. So I found myself a sign. Not far from the prison there was apparently a loudspeaker of Radio Moscow, which broadcast news at 5. Before the news they played some Communist melody. I would lean against the wall, making an effort to absorb the melody.

Well, Queen Shabbat arrived. I again found a nail with which I scraped on the wall, as I was wont to do, the two Shabbat candles, and I made the blessing over the Shabbat candles! Unfortunately, I didn't remember the whole of the Kabbalat Shabbat welcoming prayer by heart, and this pained me a great deal.

After the prayer came the meal. I drew out from among the cracks the treasures of my bread, and covered them with half of the handkerchief. I made the blessing over wine, and made the Hamotzi blessing on the bread. I ate and was satisfied. The time came for singing. I did not know any Shabbat songs at all, but every word in Hebrew, after all, is holy, so I sang the whole set of the Riga underground songs. 'Eretz Zavat Chalav Udvash'(Land flowing with milk and honey), 'David Melech Israel' (David King of Israel), 'Hine Ma Tov Uma Naim'(How good and pleasant it is), and more. One must also dance, and on my mother's side I came from a Chabad family. But the cell was narrow. Instead of dancing I began to jump back and forth and to sing. It was an exalted feeling of holy worship. A Jew sits in the cellars of the KGB and rejoices in his Shabbat. The exaltation was so great that I suddenly saw how the wall in front of me moved like a curtain. Behind the curtain I saw the walls of Jerusalem, the Jaffa Gate and the lights. I really saw them!

And then the warder began to shout 'What are you singing here? Do you think it's a rest home?' It really was Heavenly Jerusalem. I explained to him that it was Shabbat today, a holy day for Jews, and we had to rejoice. Since, following the many trials I had undergone, I had earned the reputation of a being a serious person, the warder did not get angry. He only said: 'But just don't make a lot of noise.' In the meantime the gentile went to his colleague in the shift and together they watched through the spy-hole in the door, how down there below, in the cellar, a Jew welcomed the Shabbat in spite of everything.

Such was my acquisition of the Shabbat.

Chapter 6

Kosher Life

23. THE KOSHER SALAD

Already upon my arrival at the first camp in the forests of Mordovia it was clear to me that I would try to eat only kosher food. However, decision is one thing and reality another. Therefore, I came to the camp, or more precisely, I was transported to it with a certain anxiety. Would I, in fact, succeed in keeping Kashrut?

Despite my lack of knowledge regarding Kashrut, I knew that one must avoid non-kosher ('treif') foods. I did not think about meat and milk because there is no milk in prison. They cook generally a wheat-meal porridge which, for some reason, has a blue colour. And there was also soup. They cooked the soup from potatoes and cabbage leaves (in the northern countries there are almost no worms in the cabbage). Sometimes they would add to the soup 'treif' fat.

Surprisingly, despite my lack of knowledge concerning the laws of Kashrut, I also had heard about 'Kulot' (Kula being the possibility of acting according to the lenient view), and 'Heterim' (permissions). I was also aware of the instruction which the Hafetz Chaim had given to Jewish soldiers in the Russian Army. I had also heard about the general permission of 'Pikuach Nefesh', of the preservation of life. It was convenient for Jews to act according to these Heterim, apparently, but I had determined to myself that I would need them only when there was a real danger to life.

Therefore, already in the first lesson which I gave to my student Shimon in the camp, I dwelt upon the need to keep Kashrut when eating food. Initially, Shimon rejected any possibility of realizing our desire. However, being an enterprising fellow, and after I had again stressed the importance of the matter, he found a fine solution. We appointed a 'Kashrut supervisor'.

Shimon, being a sociable person, was in contact with the Ukrainian community in the camp. These were young people who had fought against the Soviet regime for the sake of their national independence. This group viewed the State of Israel as a kind of symbol of national revival, and the rebirth of Israel spoke to their hearts. 'When we see how you have succeeded in reviving and renewing your state, we also are beginning to believe that we can establish our own state.' A light to the nations.

Thanks to this, we located one Ukrainian named Pavel, who worked in the camp kitchen. We explained to him that we avoided eating non-kosher food. This was no big news for him, since the rumour that in the camp lived a group of young Jews who observed the commandments of their faith, had become widespread. 'If you can,' we requested him, 'please remove a small portion of the soup before they add the fat, and if you can't, please warn us'.

Now the prisoners are returning from the forced labour and stand in a long line of hundreds of people next to the food distribution window. Each one inserts into the window his aluminum plate, and anxiously waits to see what they will ladle him from the big pot. Perhaps he will be lucky enough to obtain, besides water, a piece of potato as well. At last it is my turn but, to my misfortune, Pavel pokes his face out of the distribution window and gives me a warning sign. Today, there is fat in the soup. 'It is forbidden to you', Pavel goes on to say, the faithful 'Mashgiach'. Shimon and I leave the queue hungry. Today there is no food.

Actually however, we didn't die from hunger, because there was bread, and one could manage nicely on bread and water alone. Pikuach Nefesh? And also there was no danger to life. Thus, with a measure of bread, we could manage quite well, and the main thing was that we believed.

Moreover, my friend Shimon knew types of herbs that could be eaten. If cows could eat them, so could people. The camp was built over a swamp, so that the prisoners could not dig escape tunnels. Thanks to the swamp and the damp there was vegetation, and we learned to eat it. Nutritional supplements and vitamins to all intents and purposes. When we managed to find a nettle bush, we knew for certain that it had health value.

Once, during the 'salad harvesting' behind the hut, a control officer caught me and called me to come over to him. I thought that he would begin to question me why I was rummaging about in the grass. On the contrary, he pointed to the kippa on my head and demanded that I

With Prisoners of Zion Yuli Edelstein (Knesset Member) and Ida Nudel, 1989.

remove it. I refused. Thus, in close proximity to the grass affair, there 'grew' the affair of the kippa.

24. THE AFFAIR OF THE KIPPA

As I have said, already before the arrest I had decided to cover my head, as a marked expression of my Jewishness. Therefore, I bought myself a beret which I wore at home and in the streets of Riga both in winter and summer, and thus, without any prior intent, I aroused the curiosity of those around me. In response to my friends' questions concerning the significance of my permanent head covering, I would say that I was observing the tradition. Interestingly, that precisely this custom was perceived by me to be an important principle in Judaism. And perhaps I was right, because this was a demonstrative sign, and at times even embarrassing to my friends. This sign I bore as a declaration of defiance before everyone.

An hour before our hijacking attempt on the plane, my friends demanded that I remove the beret. After all, it was a strange item which might arouse the suspicion of the security men in the airfield. I refused. That I should remove the identifying sign of the people of Israel at a time of action on behalf of the people of Israel? Absolutely not! During the arrest in the airfield, when the soldiers wrestled me to the ground, and dragged me across the tarmac for interrogation, the beret fell off my head and never returned to me.

Therefore, I exchanged this honorable head covering for a handkerchief. I knotted its four corners and tightened it on my head, and thus reached the interrogation room. This strange appearance of a security prisoner, entering interrogation with a rag on his head, aroused the ire of my 'polite' interrogator. He began to tell me that this was a peculiar behavior, and was uncivilized. Therefore, instead of answering his questions about the caches of books we had hidden, I delivered to him an address about the culture of Israel and the tradition of Israel. 'It is our culture, and don't mock it.' Thus did I win the first point in the battle for my Judaism against the interrogator.

Also, when I arrived at the camp, my head was covered. That is to say, I sewed for myself and Shimon kippot from the material of prisoners' trousers, and we wandered around the camp without the warders paying any particular attention to them.

But that control officer who arrived from Moscow could well distinguish the curious thing on my head. Therefore, when he called me to come to him, he did not ask me why I was rummaging on the ground, but said:

'What is that you have on your head?'

'It's a kippa.'

And he then received from me a discourse on the duty of every Jew to wear a kippa, and on tradition in general.

'I don't care what your religion is. You can be religious, but only in your heart. Outwardly you must appear like everyone else. Prisoner, since on the list of prisoner clothing there is no mention of a kippa, you must remove it at once! And don't say that I am punishing you for observing your religion. For violating the prison regulations – you will be punished.'

I refused to remove the kippa.

'Take him to the command headquarters.'

At the headquarters the soldiers fell on me. They removed the kippa from my head, and pushed me out with a warning: 'Don't dare any more to walk around with a kippa. If we catch you again – you will be punished.'

So began a game of cat-and-mouse. We sewed more kippot for ourselves. They caught us and punished us, and we sewed kippot again, and so it went on repeatedly. The punishment wasn't too severe: solitary confinement, or reduced food ration, or cancellation of the food parcel which arrived once a year. It was possible to suffer. After all these persecutions the warders despaired. How much already could one hunt those stubborn Jews? When all was said and done, the warders were working for a wage, whereas we- for the sake of Heaven. It was clear who would win.

In the end, the warders found the weak point. The right to the annual visit. Now there arrived the day which I had been looking forward to for a whole year – a personal meeting with Father. He, ill and exhausted, arrives after a journey of thousands of kilometres to the camp in the mountains of darkness, and knocks at the gate. At once the camp commandant invites me and informs me about the meeting. Great! Finally I will see my dear father.

'But you must remove the kippa. Under no circumstances will we authorize a meeting for you when you are violating the regulations,' says the camp commandant with the quiet of a sadist, relishing every word.

'I will not remove it.'

The meeting was cancelled.

My father returned the way he had come, without receiving an explanation why the meeting with his son had been cancelled. He for sure thought to himself: 'Why did Yosef behave like that, so that because of him they cancelled the meeting? Why will he not try for me and keep the regulations?' As for me, my heart bled. My heart cried out: 'Abbah'le, my dear Father, it is not because I am blind to your suffering. It is because I have no choice.'

The warders acted thus every year.

'Remove the kippa!'
'Won't remove it!'
'The meeting is cancelled.'

On the third year of my imprisonment, on the fourth, and on the fifth, I look at the piece of cloth on my head. Was it worth for this not to see Father, my most precious possession? But, I knew that if the gentiles even think, mistakenly, that the shoelace is a holy matter to the Jews and by issuing a decree about it they will harm our Torah – the Jew will die and not remove the shoelace. And, what's more, that this is not a shoelace, but the identifying sign of the Jew. I told myself: 'Here I am representing the Jewish people. If I give in over the kippa, even for the hour of the visit, the gentiles will say that the Jews have nothing holy, Heaven forbid!'

Thus it happened that until my father's death I was not destined to see his face. That was the price that I paid for honouring Hashem.

In 1974, when he was seriously ill, my father, Moshe Ben Aharon z'l, decided to leave the watch which he had kept for me in a foreign land and to escape to the Holy Land without our parting from one another. But his strength failed him, and he died on his way to Israel. Exactly like Moshe Rabenu. It was on the eve of the fast of 17 Tammuz.

After great efforts, the Government of Israel managed to redeem his bones from the Russians and to bring him for burial on the eve of the fast of Tisha b'Av, on the Mount of Olives opposite the Temple Mount.

Father, your deeds were not in vain!

Chapter 7

Chanukah Miracles

25. CHANUKAH MIRACLES/THE CANDLE WHICH DIDN'T LIGHT

Chanukah occupies a special place in my life. First of all, because of the heroes of Israel who risked their lives for the sake of the Torah and succeeded. This was a big example for me. As a member of the Jewish underground I felt myself very close to the Maccabees. My first encounter with the Jewish people was due to Chanukah. And this is how it happened.

I was a student in the working youth high school in Riga. In our class there were quite a few Jews. Pini, who sat next to me in class, said to me: 'Next Sunday, Jewish youth will assemble for work in the cemetery in Romboli.'

The news sounded strange in my ears. Jewish youth? Was this not a general term belonging to the whole of the Jewish people, whereas we were in the Galut, in the Diaspora exile in Riga. We were really, as it says in the Book of Esther, 'a people dispersed and disparate'. We had never been together, we did not know what 'together' meant. And suddenly 'Jewish youth'? And what did it mean 'to assemble to work together'? Was it not forbidden for Jews to assemble? Nobody had the right to assembly, apart from the authorities themselves. And why in the cemetery? What could there be to do in a cemetery?

Yes, there were many questions, and they all had but one answer in the heart of the young and excited Jew: 'I must get there.' Despite the warnings of my father, who had not long ago been released from prison, I travelled there.

I got off the bus on the outskirts of the city. There were no cemeteries here and no Jews were to be seen. Just a simple gentile village. Broad fields. Houses. I hid behind the bushes near a ditch at the edge of the field, and examined the surroundings.

Suddenly – there they were! A group of people inside a field of nettles. My heart told me that they were here, the Jews. My heart told me: 'Here there is the beginning of something big in my life.' My heart leapt within me. I vaulted over the ditch and ran to join the Jews. I joined them. I did what they did. I didn't yet understand why they collected the dirt on a slope of the hill and hurled it in boxes into the field into a valley and there poured it out. Where was the cemetery? I did not ask questions.

Slowly I understood everything. The terrible truth. This field, and also the adjacent field, all of it was a cemetery or, more correctly, pits in which tens of thousands of Jews of Riga who had been murdered by the Nazis on one winter's night had been buried. It was on the eve of Chanukah 1942. In these fields the Jews had been shot and covered with clods of earth. Time had passed, the flesh had rotted. Heaven forefend! And in the ground there remained fissures. A real vale of tears. These fissures we attempted to cover and give the form of a grave, without the express permission of the authorities, half clandestinely.

I began to frequent the place every Sunday. I was there on many Sundays, year after year, and I became the work manager. A youth group formed. If, at first, Jewish youth of all ages had gathered together, a year later we had a solid group of young men and girls of the same age. As if the dead had chosen us one by one. A young man came to the edge of the surrounding wood and asked: 'Is this with the permission of the government?' 'What shall I tell you...' 'Oh, no, no. I cannot endanger myself. I want to study in the university They will disqualify me if they know that I come here.' And there were those who did not ask. They came. They worked and returned. From them there arose our nucleus.

One day we organized a silent vigil in memory of the victims. Among other things, I said:

'My friends. We have come here to help the dead. But in fact we were also dead, dry bones without the moistness of a Jew. Just look what a miracle has happened to us! Thanks to these dead people, we have got to know one another. We have become Jewish youth. We have discovered to ourselves that we belong to an oppressed people, but to a great people with a magnificent history. Can you hear what the dead are whispering to us? They are saying to us: "Learn from our experience, don't remain in the Galut. Escape from here to Eretz Israel. Lech lecha! (Go!).' Thus we rose from the dust. Really the vision of the dry bones! Thus took place the miracle of the resurrection of the Jewish People in the Galut. At the site of the holocaust in Riga which took place on the eve of the Festival of Lights.

On that same day we decided to establish a Jewish underground organization, and the aim was education. To educate as many as possible, that they should remember and know: 'We are Jews. This is not our place. We have Eretz Israel.' I wrote in the programme of the organization: 'We believe that the day will come and we will be able to leave the Galut.' Thus arose among us the belief in the redemption of Israel.

As one of the first activities, we decided to light the Chanukah candles on the graves of the murdered. To light for them a light which they had been unable to see. We built glass boxes. We obtained a lot of paraffin oil to make candles which would light for the longest time possible, and we decided to light them around the clock – a Chanukah light, a Ner Tamid, an eternal light. The activity was also necessary for the organization. In this way we would be able to recruit many youth who would join the movement through their activity.

I arrive with my companion and alight from the bus straight into the freezing cold of the winter. Darkness, fields buried in snow. The dogs barking in the village. Exactly like on that night of the tragedy. My eyes scour the darkness. Is the candle light burning?

There is something wonderful about a small candle in the darkness. It can be seen from a distance. And when I see the light I feel warmth in my heart, and I stride in the snow along the snow-covered path. They were here also before you! If to look for symbols, what could be more symbolic of the whole history of the Jewish people? In the darkness you walk by the light of the candle which they lit before you, and you will also light for those who will come after you.

But sometimes...there is no light. Perhaps someone has failed to come, or else the wind has extinguished the light. And then I go down into the snow to light a candle for those who will come after me. And this, in my opinion, is an even more appropriate symbol for us. To walk not because of the hope, but by virtue of the belief and the need of the hour.

These were the first days of Chanukah. Meeting with the Hevre (companions) around a table, lighting the candles and conversations about Israel and Eretz Israel. The time has come not to speak – but to get up and go. We got up and went. We fell into a waterless pit.

26. PUBLICIZING A MIRACLE

We had been sitting in prison already half a year after the attempted plane hijacking. The interrogation had ended. We were already sick and tired of waiting for the trial. Let it be already, and we would know what our sentence would be. Death? Life imprisonment? We signed the announcement which we had received, according to which the trial would take place on 15 November. A week before the trial they brought to the cell an additional announcement, that the trial had been postponed and would take place on 15 December. Ouf! More waiting!

Finally, this date also arrived. They got us up at 5 a.m. Each prisoner was seated in a separate vehicle. Through a slit in the side of the prison services vehicle I saw that we were travelling in a long convoy. Only in a few houses did they put the lights on when they heard the noise of the convoy, It all made a terrible impression, as if we had been given the death sentence, and now they were taking us secretly to conceal the crime which they were about to commit.

At the entrance to the court there stood dozens of soldiers and police, and rightly so. Were we not terrorists? Such a group had not been in Russia for a long while. But we considered ourselves as being temporary prisoners of war, as soldiers in a great war, thanks to the victims slain in Romboli. From them we had received the order to save the Jewish people.

The courtroom was noisy and 150 people had entered it, all of them by invitation. Select people. What could be more pleasurable than to see how Jewish blood was being shed? More interesting than sitting in a theatre.

There are three benches for the accused, to seat exactly twelve people. Each of us has been assigned a sergeant, to ensure that we do not speak with one another. The Soviets had kept us isolated from each other during all the months of interrogation because they understood that if we were together we would strengthen one another, and their intention was only to weaken us.

Despite all the precautions, my friend Arie managed to whisper to me during one of the days of the trial 'Today is the first candle of Chanukah.' Suddenly, everything became clear to me. The postponement of the trial date had occurred, because Hashem wanted us to be tried on a day on which He had wrought a miracle for His people. 'You stood by them in their time of misfortune.'

I knew that Hashem was sending me a blessing from Heaven. 'Yosef, you have been numbered among the soldiers of the Maccabees.'

I was proud and fortified. When the judge asked me: 'What actually caused you to want to escape to Israel?' I answered him as befits a descendant of the Maccabees: 'Did not Hashem give the Land of Israel to Abraham, Isaac and Jacob, and I am one of their descendants. Therefore my place is there.' The judges were stunned by such chutzpa (cheek) and called me 'a religious fanatic'.

However, this was not the main part of the miracle. The judge called each of the accused one by one, and each of us declared his wish to be in Israel. No one was afraid, and none feared the punishment. Eight Jews stood in the courtroom and declared their loyalty to the Jewish People.

For fifty years the Soviet authorities lied to the world and claimed that the Jews in their empire were loyal to the regime and were removing themselves from the ranks of the Jewish people. It was difficult for the Jews of the world to accept this. Had not the Besht (the Baal Shem Tov) and the Gra (the Vilna Gaon), the Baal Hatanya and the Hafetz Haim and all the rest emerged from these places? And suddenly darkness had descended on Jerusalem in the Galut? How could this be? But slowly the Jews became accustomed to this, and saw it as fact. They wept and regretted it. They said about the Judaism of Silence that it was fading and vanishing. And then we rose up, and from inside the court we proclaimed 'Am Israel Chai.' We were not dead. We had come back to life from the dry bones, and we were going to Eretz Israel. This was a true Pirsumei Nisa, publicizing a miracle. The Jewish world was in uproar. The Jews of Silence had come back to life! And we, in the courtroom, each of us lit the Chanukah light from our marrow and from our blood.

I remembered the candles we had lit on Chanukah in Romboli. The light from those candles lit up and aroused. Jews all over the world rose with the cry: 'Let my people go!' Thus did Chanukah become Pesach.

In Israel and in America, in France and England, and everywhere, hundreds of thousands of Jews demonstrated opposite the embassies of the wicked Russians, and they retreated. On one of the nights of Chanukah, after we had received harsh sentences, a special messenger arrived in my cell:

'Write an appeal!'

'I have to get a lawyer, to consult with.'

'There is no time. Write now.'

I sat down and wrote on a small piece of paper: 'They accuse me of betraying the motherland. My motherland is Israel. And I will not betray it. Although Russia is the land of my birth, but it is my right not to be here. Because you have prevented me from leaving Russia legally, I was forced to try and escape. Therefore, this is not a just sentence.'

He read and said: 'Is this how one writes an appeal?' Perhaps, under different circumstances, he would have thrown the paper in my face, but this time, what I didn't know then, it was the night of the Plague of the Firstborn. The international pressure reached its height, and there was an atmosphere of urgency in the air. Everything must end this night. The verdict was already prepared, but if we didn't write an appeal, how would it be possible to answer it?

The moment that the cruel regime failed in its machinations against the Jews, and when its schemes were uncovered and visible to all, its leaders tried to hide themselves like a wounded animal, and quickly. Brezhnev summoned to him the head of the spy services. 'Who has been so utterly stupid as to attempt to set a trap for the Jews? Now we have fallen into the trap, and the whole world is shouting that our Jews want to emigrate to Israel.'

That same night they punished the perpetrators of the plot to catch the Jews 'in the act'. The stupid officers who thought to trick the Jews received a special treatment: they were all reduced in ranks, and fired from their work and exiled to Siberia. The next day the Supreme Court of Justice sat in Moscow and reduced all of our sentences. After a few days, it was decided by the regime leadership to begin to give exit visas to the Jews. This was a Chanukah miracle. We knew nothing about the great events because we were still in solitary confinement.

A year after the trial they took us out to a forced labour camp. They placed each one of us in a separate cell compartment on the prison train. We were labelled 'extremely dangerous security prisoner' – what an honour! When I finally sat down on the bench in the compartment, I opened a bag with letters sent to me during the year. But I had not received any of them because of the isolation. I now read the first letter and couldn't believe my eyes.

It read as follows: "I am writing to you from the Russian border. We have received Aliya emigration visas. Hevra, it's thanks to you. Thank you!'

And another letter, and another. And finally, a telegram from my sisters: 'We have received exit visas.' It was a wonderful feeling of thanksgiving to Hashem for the loving-kindness He had shown us. Instead of being shot we had been granted to see the miracle of the Exodus from Egypt in our time. Although we were being transported to the land of darkness, our brethren of Israel were leaving boldly with pride.

I descend from the plane which brought me from Russia to Israel, 18.2.81. Next to me, my sister Rivka Drori.

27. THE CHANUKAH LIGHT IN THE WATCHTOWERS

On the first Chanukah in the forced labour camp we decided to celebrate the festival openly. To this end, I wrote to the camp commander demanding that we be given the possibility to meet together. At the same time we began to equip ourselves in preparation for the festival. One Lithuanian, with knowledge of carpentry, from among the opponents to the Russian occupation, made a small wooden Chanukia candelabra which, instead of branches, used nails on which to stick the candles, and the candles handmade from wax which I stole from the plant storeroom. Apparently, someone informed on me, and the warders conducted a search in the prisoners' implements. My turn came. The Chanukiah was lying hidden in the sack. I reacted as if in anger: 'What do you suspect me of? I don't have anything?' And while speaking I emptied the whole sack demonstratively, so that the contents were scattered in every direction. I immediately stood between the policeman and the sock in which the Chanukah Menorah was hidden. Whilst I engaged him in conversation, I pushed the Chanukiah under a wooden shelf. That was a small miracle before the festival.

Right before the festival we noticed a lorry entering the plant to take away the produce of the plant which the prisoners had produced, while on the floor of the lorry some potatoes were scattered. Hashem had also sent us 'latkes' (potato pancakes). Now it only required a little heroism, because jumping into a lorry was considered as an escape attempt. Shimon risked his life and sprang into the lorry. I stood below and received the potatoes from him. There were more than ten of them, with which Shimon attempted to prepare the latkes in the stove of the hut. At the same time, Zeev hired from one gentile of the camp aristocracy his bed, located at the corner of the hut.

Before the start of the festival, the camp commandant summoned me. He was red in the face with anger that the Jews had assumed that he, the known anti-Semite, would allow us to sit together. 'Don't you dare, and if you do we shall place you all in solitary confinement.'

We felt each other to be the sons of Matityahu the Maccabee, and we didn't care at all about the punishment anticipated for the sin of welcoming the festival. Therefore, we sat down, and I respectfully lit the candle with a blessing. We began to eat latkes. We also had a dreidl (a four-sided spinning top) and we played with it, and gave candies as prizes. The truth was that we were a bit on edge in view of the promised clash with the inspectors, but they didn't come. We went out to the camp yard and sang songs of the motherland, everything that we knew how to sing in Hebrew. The warders that evening didn't appear at all in the camp. This was like a kind of Pirsumei Nisa since all the gentiles saw us celebrating the festival in violation of the camp regulations and with no harm.

However, a real miracle occurred precisely in the last year of my imprisonment, on the eleventh Chanukah.

28. CHANUKAH ON MOUNT SINAI

After three years of imprisonment in Vladimir Prison, I was returned to the previous camp, Number 36. Twice Chai (18, number symbolizing life and luck), I said to myself as was my wont. In every number I saw, I searched for meaning.

Meanwhile, thanks to the struggle of World Jewry, my companions from the Leningrad trial were released and immigrated to Eretz Israel, whereas I was still in prison, As Anatoly Sharansky explained to me, when he was in Chistopol Prison, there was an agreement for the release of Prisoners of Zion in exchange for ratifying the Disarmament Agreement between the USA and the Soviet Union of that time. As a trust-building step, the first group of Prisoners of Zion were released before the ratification, whereas I was counted with the 'prestigious' group of Prisoners of Zion whose release was considered as a gift to the West.

Reception in New York after the release, with Elie Wiesel.

As our luck would have it, and in the wake of the Soviet invasion of Afghanistan in 1980, the agreement was not ratified by the American Senate, which protested in this way at the invasion. Thus, I remained stuck in jail, while the rest of my companions were breathing the air of Eretz Israel. For some reason, the non-Jewish prisoners sought to persuade me in two directions. Firstly, that I had not been released because I observed the Mitzvot, and the Russians hated such people. The obvious conclusion was that it was preferable to be secular. Possibly these prisoners, 'concerned for my welfare', had been sent by the KGB. The second tendency was to convince me that the State of Israel had forgotten me, and apparently they expected that, as a result of this, I would betray the State of Israel. It was, of course, very funny. I had long ago decided that nobody, nor even any state, owed me anything. All that I did was because it was my duty to Hashem and to my people, and I didn't need any prize. After all, my connection with Hashem was the biggest prize of all.

I prepared myself that perhaps I might never see Eretz Israel, and I planned that, upon my release, I would immediately return to Jewish underground activity. Perhaps I would manage, before the next arrest, to find a kosher Jewess, for example from Bokhara, and this too was not mandatory. Therefore, I did not preoccupy myself at all with the question of why they had not released me. It was clear that this was the will of Hashem, and that he had left me here to accomplish His mission.

And indeed, the moment they brought me back to the previous labour camp in the Ural mountains, I was informed that there was a young Jew in the camp who wanted to learn Hebrew, and also that he had been accused of attempting to take hostages in order to exchange them for me, Sharansky and Ida Nudel. He was a young man and in my eyes not too serious. His name was Vadim, a name that rang in my ears like 'Din' (judgement), and so I changed his name to 'Dan'.

I brought with me from the prison quite a few holy books that I had come by after my other companions had been released. At the entrance to labour camp Number 36 they placed me in quarantine for two weeks, and only after that was I sent to work. But the suitcase with the books they didn't give me, because the duty officer didn't know what to do with them. Then, a daring thought occurred to me. When the duty officer was changed, I came to his replacement and pretended that they had to give me back the suitcase. Apparently, in the log-book nothing had been written about it, and therefore the officer, quite a primitive but good-hearted man, asked me if the books had already been examined? I answered that I thought they had been. I received the suitcase, and hid it when it turned out several days later that the suitcase had not been checked. The officer came to me furiously, and asked me why I had tricked him. Again I feigned innocence, and said that apparently there was some mistake. With that, for the time being, the matter ended.

I had a Hebrew study book by Shlomo Kodesh which had been smuggled from Israel, and with its help I began to teach Hebrew. Apparently, some 'Shtinkers' informed on me, and I was summoned to the secret police office inside the prison. The KGB representative informed me that by my teaching Hebrew I was committing a transgression, because the Hebrew language didn't really exist. This was a language that served political-Zionist ends only. Interestingly, at that time Hebrew teachers were also being persecuted throughout the Soviet Union, and I, who knew nothing of this, acted like them. I simply ignored it. If I was afraid to teach Hebrew what should I live for?

Meanwhile, there was a new development. They put Dan into the inner prison of the camp, the B.O.R., the solitary confinement punishment cell. I looked for a way to help him, at least with food. I began to collect bread and pass it to him, because the hunger there was greater. As part of the wider search after food accumulations, the warders decided to conduct a search also in the storeroom. They demanded that I identify my belongings and show them to the warders. Obviously, I did not bring the warders to the 'sacred' suitcase, because in the storeroom there were many suitcases of prisoners, big piles of them, and it wasn't too difficult to confuse them. In short, they didn't find anything with me.

As we left the storeroom (apparently due to informing) they suddenly asked me: 'Is this your suitcase?' My heart fell within me. They had found the treasure! Immediately, the warders opened the suitcase and understood that they were on the right track. They said they would send the books to Moscow, for translating, and it was clear that the treasure was going to go down the drain. I left the storeroom with the feeling that I was completely lost. Again I was required to fight for what was important for me above all, important like life itself. But where would I get the strength from? My strength had failed due to the continuous 137-month struggle.

But I knew that Hashem was giving me another test. Help arrived from an unexpected source. I had become friendly not long before with a Ukrainian fighter named Zinovy Krasyevsky. He had fought in the forests against the Red Army which had conquered the Western Ukraine, and had been sentenced to 25 years' imprisonment. He had a very special story, but two things stood out in him above all else. First of all, he didn't know how to despair. In every difficult situation in which he found himself, Zinovy found some positive side. In this we resembled one another, and on this basis we grew close. He certainly admired the State of Israel as an example for the revival of his own nation. He also could give people credit. He told me more than once that he was amazed by the power of my struggle for the Jewish people, and his confidence in my ability to continue the struggle was so firm that it looked to me like a Chillul Hashem (a desecration of the Divine Name) in the eyes of the gentiles if I did not recommence the struggle for the holy books. Really, as it is said: 'Then they will say among the nations.' I thought also that Moshe Rabenu, Alav Hashalom (may he rest in peace), always turned to Hashem with the claim that the nations will say, Heaven forbid, that He does not help us.

From a self-scrutiny I concluded that the Chillul Hashem of the confiscation of the holy books had been decreed upon me, because for many years prior to my arrest I had not observed fasts, and now

The day after my release Prime Minister Menachem Begin welcomed me. 1981.

Hashem wanted me to give them back to Him in kind. Thus, a strange thing had happened. By virtue of doing charity and the desire to give bread to my friend, I had lost the holy books. But in actual fact this was a gain, because I found in myself a new power. By overcoming my weakness I had learned to give way and to exercise self-restraint.

And so I set forth on a new campaign. The only way to fight was by declaring a hunger strike. It certainly was inappropriate to begin the strike without informing my friends in Israel. Once more a way was found with the help of Zinovy. He was due to be 'released' and to be sent to a place of exile in eastern Siberia, at a distance of some 500 kilometres from any big city. In any event, one could somehow get to that place and leave it without any special permit, but under supervision of the KGB, the Committee for State Security. Therefore, I arranged with him that the moment that his wife reached him, he would give her details about the method of transferring the information, and she would bring the news to the Aliya activists in Moscow. The moment that the news was received, our friends would see to it to send it to Israel and the USA, to the UN Human Rights Commission, and, at the

At the meeting in the White House. Discussion about the situation of the Jews in the Soviet Union. Right after my release in 1981. On my left in the picture, President Ronald Reagan and Vice-President Bush Sr.

same time, they would send me as confirmation a postcard with a national symbol on it and containing some greeting, so that it would be approved by the authorities. And so it was.

I can surmise how complex was this mission entrusted to the Ukrainian woman from a village in the Carpathian mountains. However, she carried it out in all its details, so that one day I received a postcard with the portrait of the Communist leader, Vladimir Lenin, and on the postcard greetings for the October Revolution! I do not know if the censorship, which was charged with examining prisoners' mail, wondered as to the meaning of this postcard, but for me the message was clear and joyful: the news about my plan had arrived and I must begin the hunger strike.

Interestingly enough, I had not thought to also plan my own confirmation of receipt of the postcard, so trusting were we in each other that we knew that the moment the decision was made she would not return empty-handed.

I wrote a letter to the camp commandant, and announced that I was embarking on a hunger strike until my holy books were returned to me. The significance of such a declaration was the readiness of the hunger striker to die gradually, within forty days. The truth is that without drinking water one dies within a week, but that was too short a time to apply the pressure. I decided to go on a hunger strike in which only water was permitted. The conditions of such a strike were known and accepted, and it, of course, did not include drinking juices, tea, or any other nourishing drink. Moreover, if anyone of the strikers was caught drinking a drink of that kind, he would immediately be denounced publicly as a cheat and be in disgrace.

Thus I entered the first test circuit. Suddenly there were good friends who advised me to be clever, and to exploit the fact that nobody would know whether I ate in secret. Some of these 'friends' were agents of the regime, and their intention was to make me fail. But also the advice of the real fiends was unacceptable to me, and this was not only out of fear in case they would catch me 'in the act'. I felt that this struggle for the holy books must be pure and devoid of any personal taint. Only if I would be really ready to sacrifice my life, or at least to suffer, did I have the chance that Hashem would help me. It was clear to me that the struggle I was waging was not against any particular officer, but it was a case here of an act which, if successful, would bring the redemption closer.

And so twenty-one days passed, in the course of which I had to report every day for work, otherwise I would have been declared an evader, a declaration which would have given the authorities a pretext to break me for a breach of discipline and not on the main aspect of the struggle. Hashem gave me the strength, and thus I would report daily and complete my quota of work. The truth is that after three days of distress in the stomach, my body got used to the new reality and stopped demanding that I feed it.

After these twenty-one days, I was summoned by the camp 'doctor' for an inspection, and I was supposed to emit such odours from the mouth that would testify to the fact that I was in an advanced state of biological death. I received from the doctor the confirmation that indeed I was hunger-striking, and as a 'bonus' I was sent at once to solitary confinement, although with the preferential conditions of a hunger striker: I was allowed to lie down and to have pencil and paper in the cell. The real 'bonus' was that I was placed in a cell close to my pupil Dan.

We at once renewed our studies by using the main waste pipe which connected the toilet bowls in the cells, as a kind of open 'phone line'. They were not exactly toilet bowls, but holes in the floor for doing one's business, which were covered over. There only remained to knock on the wall to announce the start of the lesson, to go to the hole to remove the cover and begin. This kind of contact between prisoners was, of course, absolutely forbidden, and the warders were equipped with soft slippers so as to muffle the sound of their steps, and to make it easier for them to hunt us and catch us 'in the act'. However, our willpower was, of course, stronger than their sadistic inclination. We watched from behind the door every movement of theirs. When they got tired and returned to the command room to drink tea and chat, the time for learning had arrived.

From a previous experience of hunger strikes I knew that it was very important for me to maintain my morale and not pity myself at all. There were those who within a few days would lie down and feel they were going to die, and thereby undoubtedly play into the hands of the enemy. I acted quite the opposite. I followed a daily schedule which began, of course, with the morning prayer of several hours, then gymnastics, reading and writing. The warders were amazed by my durability. One of them said to me:

'Young man, you are surely cheating. I don't know how, but it is clear to me that you eat.'

'But you are the one who is inspecting me, and you know that no one can come near me without a search.'

'You are right. But explain to me how is it that you almost don't lie on the bed? I have seen many hunger strikers and they were all flat on their beds already after the first two days of their strike.'

The truth is that it was a miracle. Apart from my decision to endure at all costs, I received the strength from the very fact that in my struggle there was no personal connection, on the contrary, on the personal side I didn't want to hunger strike at all. I did it for Hashem, and He helped me. Two weeks after they placed me in the solitary confinement, my friend Dan said to me: 'Yosef, I know that you observe the Mitzvot, and I want to learn from you not only the Hebrew language but also everything to do with the Mitzvot.' This was great news. I immediately made a decision that I would write for him all that I remembered from the Chumash, and I sat down to write. It really was a gift from G-d, to sit in the cell, in a strike for the sake of holy books, and to write words of Torah for a captive Jew, to think about the Torah and to live the Torah. As I wrote to my sisters in Eretz Israel, 'I feel like Moshe Rabenu on Mount Sinai.'

The primitive local censorship certainly was not capable of getting to the bottom of my thinking, nor was it capable of solving the clue and understanding that my hunger strike was already forty days old. But it was also doubtful whether my friends in Israel understood that this was not simply a numerical clue, but that I really was on a very high level of spiritual exaltation.

Hashem showed me an additional way to transmit the Torah to Dan. These were days of winter in the snow-bound Ural mountains. According to the regulations I was allowed to go out each day for a half-hour stroll in the inner prison yard. The yard was very narrow. Barely wide enough for one person, and still more congested due to the large amount of snow that had fallen on it. It was, therefore, natural for me to ask the guard in the watchtower to give me implements to clear the little yard, and I collected the snow exactly below the watchtower. And so I had clear room to skip, which I was cleverly able to do in this narrow space. The guard looked down from above and laughed at my gymnastics. The poor fellow did not understand that each time I came near to the pile of snow under his watchtower and stretched my hands in gymnastics, I was making with the hand a recess in the snow, and in the next round placed inside that same hole a section from the Torah which I had remembered to copy during the day.

I also found a red string which was in the sack which, ten years previously, my father, may he rest in peace, had given me, and with this string I would indicate to Dan the location of the treasure. Then would come his turn to go out for a 'stroll', and to take out from the snow the secret 'message'.

To the Torah words I also added a Hebrew lesson. The lesson comprised a short story, a small dictionary, a grammatical analysis and homework. In this way I prepared a whole textbook (when Dan was released from the prison he continued teaching with its help Jews in the nearby city, and at the start of the 1990s he sent the little book to me in Israel. Unfortunately, the book got lost. By mistake someone had thrown it away.)

Then the great day arrived. On the 56th day of the hunger strike the camp commandant came to my cell and told me angrily: 'Are you still continuing to harm our state?' It was amazing. I, a miserable prisoner, barely alive, locked away in the bottom of the pit, and this officer, symbolizing a military power, tells me that I am harming his state! My joy knew no bounds. I understood that the wicked ones had received a blow from our Jewish brothers. And this was indeed the case. The news of my hunger strike had reached the table of an American Jew named Senator Kempelman, the head of the Human Rights Commission in Congress. When the subject of violation of human rights came up on the discussion table with the Russians, he stood up and said: 'How dare you talk about human rights, when in your solitary confinement there rots a young Jew who is hunger striking because you confiscated his holy books!' The Russian representative was at a loss how to respond. The prison authorities had certainly not updated the diplomats. Immediately, a question was sent from Washington to Moscow. 'Is Mendelevich really hunger striking for that? Idiots, stop at once! It is ruining all our propaganda!'

And so the camp commandant came running to me immediately after receiving a panic-stricken phone call from Moscow, seeking to find a way to end the affair. I didn't know the details of what was going on, but it was clear to me that there was here Siata Dishmaya, Divine Intercession, and therefore I spoke with the officer from a sense of power, and I set conditions for ending the strike. At my demand they brought Dan to my cell, and in the presence of a KGB representative I handed him the Hebrew textbook. I received authorization that Dan could use the book undisturbed. It seems to me that it was the first case in history that the Soviet authorities gave permission to learn Hebrew in prison from a book printed in Israel. I also received back my books.

It was a tremendous victory. Never had a prisoner defeated the prison camp management. When I emerged from the solitary, all the prisoners cheered. They tried to understand how such a thing had happened, so that they perhaps would succeed by the same method. But in vain! This secret of a Chosen People, the secret of the unity of Israel and the guarantee of Israel for one another, cannot be transferred to anyone else.

These were the days of Chanukah 1981. Whilst I was still in the solitary I tried to observe the Mitzvah of lighting the Chanukah light, to make candles from the strings of the sack which my father had given me. I watched with heavy heart how the fire consumed the strings within seconds, and I was unable to observe the Mitzvah.

The light did arise, but not from the candles. From a small cell there came out again the light of eternal Israel, and it was a Pirsumei Nisa and a light unto the nations. Its beginning was with the candles I had lit in the valley of death at Romboli, and it reached its peak in the courtroom in Leningrad.

Chapter 8

Redemption

29. FROM SLAVERY TO FREEDOM

The role of the Jewish People is to be a light unto the nations, as it is said 'For out of Zion shall go forth the Torah and the Word of the Lord from Jerusalem.' Hashem placed me in forced-labour camps in the Ural Mountains to radiate abroad from there light to the nations. I did not do so intentionally. From my soul and by my nature I wanted to do good to everyone.

I sat in the Chistopol Prison on the shores of the great Volga River. It was impossible to see the river from the behind the bars of my cell window. Instead, I saw the faces of my fellow-prisoners in the cell who I had not chosen to be my cell-mates. But we had no option – we had to live together. The cell was small. Six people in a cell. In the centre was a table. On the side opposite the table was the toilet bowl. A narrow place. In order to stretch our legs we had to take turns. Each one went at the time allotted to him in the narrow passage between the table and the prisoners' beds. No room even for two.

The additional problem – smoking. People under tension want to smoke. But others cannot stand the pungent smell of the tobacco they distributed in the prison, apparently in order to poison us. And so it was decided among the prisoners that it was permitted to smoke only half an hour before noon and half an hour after noon. During the smoking a prisoner had to sit on the second level of the iron beds.

In every cell I was in, I instinctively tried to create a family atmosphere. Thanks to this, in every cell they asked me to be a sort of 'cell manager', in charge of the cell order and the distribution of the food portions.

One day, they introduced into our cell a new person, an elderly and unfriendly dentist. He had no friends in the cell. He was a stranger to every one of us freedom fighters. He was nervous and a heavy smoker. Once, an interesting conversation arose between us. in which the dentist also participated. I suddenly noticed that he was exploiting the conversation, and smoking there on the second level outside the allotted time. I remarked to him sarcastically 'You are exploiting our good-heartedness and robbing us of our air.' I saw that he was very hurt. Perhaps I had been too sharp. Then he said: 'You don't like me, so I'm issuing a boycott. I won't speak with anyone again.' I thought to myself: 'How can this ugly and unfriendly person demand that anyone should like him? We have been many years in this stinking cell. And he even talks about liking?' I looked at him. He really did look very miserable.

But he was right, I said to myself. Everyone needs love. For that is exactly the torture which the KGB had prepared for us – that we should hate one another. Truly, I was guilty. I had hurt him. I suddenly felt a deep sorrow. I had caused another person hurt! Because of me he was suffering. It was clear to me that I had to right the wrong that I had caused him. I had to prove to him that we did love him. The other cell-mates couldn't care less about the boycott that he had issued against us, whereas I thought how hard it was for him not to talk with anyone.

Therefore, since then, at every opportunity I tried to give him the impression of affection and caring towards him. Since I was in charge of the cleanliness and distribution of the food, I was able to accomplish this without discriminating against the others, but at every opportunity I would emphasize that he had equal rights. I tried to guess in advance what would be most convenient for him in relation to each and every small thing connected with our miserable existence in the cell. It is always possible to make one's fellow man feel that one considers him and cares about him.

The dentist asked the prison commandant to transfer him to another cell. One day they called him to go out with his personal belongings. He rapidly collected the few belongings he had, and stood by the door with his back to us. Suddenly, before going out, he turned to us and said-'You are all creeps. Only Mendelevich is a real man.' Then I knew that I had emerged from slavery to freedom.

30. NOT BY BREAD ALONE

At the end of the Passover Seder, the 'Sefirat HaOmer' (Counting of the Omer) begins. A farmer goes to his field and gathers sheaves of wheat. I also had a Sefirat HaOmer in prison.

I have already told how, after the Passover Seder in jail, all my comrades from the 'Leningrad trial' were released, while I alone remained in prison. As it is written in Torah about the Patriarch Jacob 'and Jacob remained alone' in order to meet and struggle with Esau's guardian angel, so it was with me. A rumour about the unexpected release of my comrades (they would have had to remain in prison for another few years had they not been released) made a big impression on all the prisoners. It caused them to dream dreams that they too might be released unexpectedly. They did not understand or know that the release of my comrades was not a chance event, but the result of a continuous struggle of the Jewish people for the Prisoners of Zion.

I have not mentioned that with me and Hillel in the cell was a young Ukrainian man, Genia. Previously, he had been together with Natan Sharansky and had learned a bit of Hebrew from him, so that when he joined us he was already a little connected to the Jews. Therefore, we invited him to sit with us at our Passover Seder.

The news of the release affected him exceptionally. He was in prison due to the fact that when he had been under arrest for theft, he had managed to escape and board a plane in the guise of an ordinary citizen. He had been holding two apples in his hands, and he threatened the

With President Chaim Herzog, presenting him with my book *Operation Wedding*, 1985.

crew that they were explosives which he would set off if they did not fly him to Finland. The pilot gave in and flew him to Helsinki. Genia did not know that there was an agreement between the Soviet Union and Finland to extradite escapees without giving them political refugee status. Therefore, the Finnish authorities extradited Genia back to Russia and he was sentenced to 13 years in prison, Apparently, his story resembled ours in a grotesque way. Everything was similar, except for the significant difference that he had escaped from the criminal punishment whereas we had done so in order to bring freedom to our people.

Therefore, Genia began to fantasize that he too might be released. Perhaps because he was sick? Genia became sick. He had a high temperature. He apparently knew how to feign illness. I called the doctor, but the doctor was not impressed by Genia's 'illness'. But he was a determined young man and did not give up. Shabbat arrived. I got up in the morning and began to pray the Sabbath morning prayer. I did not have a Siddur, but I remembered by heart. During the prayer I heard Genia tearing paper. I was afraid that he was tearing a personal letter of mine, but I must not interrupt my prayers. I tried to concentrate on my prayer. Only when I had finished did I go to the place where before the entry of the Sabbath I had left my letter. It was a letter of complaint to the Chief Prosecutor of the Soviet Union to the effect that the KGB had confiscated all the letters that my family sent me and that I didn't receive any letters. I had prepared the letter in order to hand it on Sunday to the Prison administration. I found my letter torn into little pieces. I asked Genia 'why did you tear up my letter?' He lay on his bunk and smiled a ferocious smile.'What? You didn't tear up your letter?'

I understood that Genia was beginning a new scenario by making out that he was going crazy. And then, according to his plan, they would take him to the asylum and from there he could escape or be released. It was a very unpleasant Shabbat. When the Sabbath ended in the evening, I decided that I had to get out of the cell. Perhaps, in order to prove that he was really crazy, Genia would kill me or do something else in order to win an early release. I did not wish to be a victim of his devilry. I also knew that if I asked to be moved to another cell, the prison administration would not agree, because they would understand that I was not happy, and that was exactly what they wanted.

My plan was simple. In the evening there was change of watch shifts. At the time of the change of shifts they opened the cells, and the warders went from cell to cell counting the prisoners. Therefore, when they opened the door of my cell I fled from the cell and began to run along the prison corridor. The warders pursued me. I gripped the bars of the corridor and they struggled with me. Other prisoners heard the sound of the struggle and began to beat their metal plates on the doors of the cells. There was a tremendous noise throughout the whole prison. In brief, I kicked up a whole rumpus there. They had no choice and they placed me in solitary confinement. They punished me with 15 days in solitary.

The following day, a KGB man came and interrogated me about the reason for my escape attempt. I decided that I could not reveal the true reason. I could not provide any detail about another prisoner. Perhaps they would punish him? I said, 'I will not divulge the reason. But under no circumstances will I return to the cell.'

So I spent 15 days in solitary. I had many experiences there. Among other things, it made me very angry that they restricted me in my food. Each time they gave me a few slices of bread, and that was all. I felt like some animal whose owners decided how much food to give me, and I had no freedom of choice. Precisely there in solitary the situation most oppressed me. It was as if I were a slave.

Suddenly I had an idea. True, they were limiting me, and not giving me more, but I can express my freedom by eating less! And so I did. I did not eat all the bread they gave me and I left a slice on the side uneaten. Although I was hungry, the feeling that I was not a slave, and that I decided for myself, gave me strength and a feeling of joy for I had defeated my body.

The outcome of this saving was that, at the end of my stay in solitary, I had collected two pounds of bread. This I brought to my new cell with another prisoner. I offered the bread to this prisoner. He did not ask me where I had got it from. Generally, when a prisoner returns from solitary other prisoners give him a little extra because in solitary there is real hunger. But this prisoner was so hungry that he didn't think for a moment. He fell upon my symbol of freedom at once and wolfed it down. Thus began the daily ceremony. Every day I left him a part of my portion. This young man was a freedom fighter for his people who were under Soviet occupation. There were only two of us and so we talked a lot. He told about his people, and I about the Jewish people. Gradually it became clear that this 'freedom fighter' was not prepared to recognize that the Jewish people were deserving of respect. He was quite simply an anti-Semite.

During one loud argument he said to me that the Jews exploit the weakness of other nations in order to gain control over them.

'Here, you know that I wish to eat bread and you give me bread in order to take control of me!' This was such an idiotic thought that I could not believe my ears! I examined myself, Had I indeed given him bread in order to enjoy a feeling of supremacy? Absolutely not! And in any case, who had compelled this freedom fighter to eat my bread? And if he felt that I was abusing him in such a manner, then he shouldn't take bread from me any more. But both to take, and also to hate?

The situation was so paradoxical that I decided that I was no longer able to share a cell with him. I demanded to be moved. Apparently, the administration understood that I did not give up easily, so they at once moved me to another cell. The young man was astounded. He had not anticipated that I would act immediately. 'What, are you leaving?' Apparently, he was sorry to be losing my portion of bread...

It is written in the Torah 'For not by bread alone shall a man live but by everything that comes out from the mouth of Hashem shall he live.' (Deuteronomy, 8, 3) I learned this verse not from the Torah but from life.

31. A LIGHT UNTO THE NATIONS

'I the Lord, in My grace, have called you, and I have grasped you by the hand and created you and appointed you a covenant-people, a light unto the nations.' Isaiah 42

In the camp, our group of those who had fought for the rights of the Jewish people met Jews who had fought for 'Communism with a human face'. They would say to us that we were not right in our struggle, for if we fought for the democratic freedom of the Russian people, in the end it would be good also for the Jews. 'How is it that you don't understand that it is impossible to solve your particular problems without overall democratization? We also do not like the Soviet regime. But we did not want to interfere in a matter in which we are not involved.' Deep in my heart I felt that, by means of our struggle, we would also bring freedom to other peoples. And so it was.

All over the world the Jewish people fought for the Jews in the Soviet Union. There was no more powerful movement in the world for human rights than the struggle for freedom of emigration from the Soviet Union. In this struggle the Soviet regime learned to its cost that it could no longer withstand the free world and it disintegrated. One may rightly say that the Berlin Wall fell due to the struggle of the Jewish People for our national rights. The Ukraine became free as did Kazakhstan, Latvia, Hungary. All the experts on Soviet history agree on this point. And this is the meaning of the concept: 'Jews are a light to the Nations.' We brought freedom not only to ourselves but to all the nations who were under Soviet occupation.

'And the People of Israel went out highhandedly, boldly,'

32. PASSOVER ON PURIM

When the hunger-strike days were over, I was hospitalized in the camp hospital. This hut was intended for death rather than for healing, but at least they didn't send me to work, and they also gave me food to eat. There, in the 'hospital', a thought occurred to me. I said to myself: 'Perhaps I have already done all that I can do here, and the time has come to immigrate to Eretz Israel.' Although until now the feeling was that I was on a mission, I suddenly felt that it had ended. However, things turned out a little differently.

After the hospital I was sent again to work in the plant. It was hard work because one had to haul bundles of iron wires, each weighing sixty kilos. One evening, as I was working in the plant, there arrived two officers who I didn't know and told me to return to the living quarters and to pack my belongings. Meaning that they were transferring me to another place. But where to, and why?

So, in the middle of the night, they took me in an open jeep among the trees in a thick forest. A guard dog sat behind me, breathing heavily as if wishing to create a layer of insulation for my ears. Had this been in the days of Stalin, I would think that they were taking me for annihilation.

This was not the case. We arrived at a railway station, and I was placed in a carriage wearing a long raincoat which covered my handcuffs. My escorts pointed to their loaded revolvers and warned: 'Be a good boy!' I was. I enjoyed meeting the ordinary Russian people – workers, farmers and simple tramps. There was in this encounter the scent of freedom, which I had long ago forgotten. All of them had chosen a destination to travel to without asking anyone. A dream!

Meanwhile, we arrived at the provincial city of Perm and from there they flew me to Moscow. More precisely, to the Lefortovo prison facilities of the KGB. Without saying a word or giving any explanation, they put me into a cell and forgot about me. Complaints to the advocacy and demands to explain the reason for the transfer did not help. There was no answer. I suspected that they wished to interrogate me about how I had managed to pass the information regarding my hunger strike. Had not this act harmed the interests of Russia and sullied its name? The Soviets were liable to take revenge. Oy, how stressful! I was already sick and tired of it all. The burden was oppressive.

Thus, two weeks passed in anxious waiting. One morning I got up and, as usual, began to pray the Shacharit morning prayer. I ate a bit of bread and sat down on the mattress to think and study the fate of the Jewish people at the end of the nineteenth century. Why had the mass assimilation begun? What could have been done and what didn't the leaders do? Suddenly the heavy door of the cell opened:

'Who here is Mendelevich?'

'I am.'

'Pack your belongings.'

This meant that they were transferring me to another cell. More runaround. But when the door closed another warder fell on me.

'Idiot, why did you take belongings?'

'They told me to.'

'They didn't. Leave them here.'

No use trying to understand them. At a run they took me upstairs to the interrogation rooms. They put me in a big room. Many high-ranking officers were sitting there. It didn't look like an interrogation. One lieutenant-colonel stood up. In his hand was a sheet of paper, and he read:

'Decision of the Supreme Soviet:

Due to wicked behavior of the most dangerous criminal, Yosef Mendelevich, contrary to the moral values of the Soviet people the Supreme Soviet rules -

1. To annul the citizenship of the criminal Mendelevich.
2. To expel Mendelevich from the sovereign territory of the Soviet Union.
3. In the event that Mendelevich shall return to the territory of the state, he will be immediately arrested to serve out his sentence.'

I listened, not believing what my ears were hearing. I blurted out 'Baruch Hashem.'

'What did you say?'

'I thank G-d for the miracle He has done for me.'

'Scoundrel. They are expelling him from his motherland, and he is joyful!'

'Russia is not my motherland. On the contrary, you are expelling me from foreign soil to the motherland.'

'Good, enough, we have already heard enough. Take the criminal Mendelevich, to shower, to shave, to put on nice clothes and to expel him from here.'

The clothes were already ready in a suitcase. A black suit, hat and coat. Regal clothes. They put me into a fine car and we began to drive. On the sides police were escorting me on motorbikes. The escort, a lieutenant–colonel, said to me: 'See, they are honouring you like royalty.' And truthfully, on that day I felt that I belonged to the royal seed of Joseph when they brought him out of the pit, dressed him in fine clothing and brought him before the king. I, too, was travelling to the palace of the King of Kings – to Eretz Israel.

We reached the airfield and before I boarded the plane, I said to the lieutenant-colonel: 'Eleven years ago you arrested me in an

With the Chief Rabbi Mordechai Eliahu at the wedding of my daughter, Shlomzion Chaya, in 2006.

airfield so that I would not emigrate to Israel. Now, with your own hands, you have brought me to an airfield so that I shall emigrate to Israel. You have to admit that you made a big mistake.' The officer looked at me and said: 'We did not know that you had such willpower in you.'

Thus, almost naively, he uttered the big truth. However, it was not only our willpower. We were weak nothings. But we knew how to connect with the will of our Father In Heaven, and thanks to this we had been able to resist and overcome the great power.

Several hours flight passed, and at night the plane landed in Lod Airport. I descended from the plane into the arms of my sisters, Eva and Rivka. I was worn out and exhausted with all the excitement, like a dead man returning from Heaven with a joy that was not his. As I stood in the belly of the plane, the newspapermen asked me:

'How do you want to see the people of Israel, and why have you come?' Was this not what I had asked myself more than once. At once I answered: 'A holy nation and kingdom of priests.' I asked those around me: 'What day is it today?' They answered me: 'Don't you know? It's Purim Katan (minor Purim) today.'

I recalled that, when I was still in the underground, I published a newspaper, and I, as editor, wrote in it an editorial called 'Purim and Pesach', in which I compared the salvation of Purim to the redemption of Passover, and I had preferred Pesach.

The Holy One Blessed Be He taught me not to belittle His festivals and the miracles He wrought for the People of Israel, and He had done me 'the Nahafoch Hu' – he had turned the general Purim Katan into my personal Passover day of redemption, and on the day I recite the 'Hallel' prayer of praise and thanksgiving to the Almighty.

'...And for Your miracles which are with us every day'.

33. TEFILLIN, TEHILIM AND TILIM

(Phylacteries, Psalms and Rockets)
The story of a miracle which happened during
Operation Protective Edge

In 1980, Russia was still under a tyrannical Soviet rule. In spite of all the persecution, a religious awakening began among the Jews of the Soviet Union. A special envoy of Rabbi Menachem Mendel Schneerson (the Lubavitcher Rebbe) arrived in the Soviet Union. He was surprised

Praying with Jewish pupils in a forest near Kiev, 2012.

Giving a lesson in Gemara in Machon Meir Yeshiva Institute in Jerusalem, 2015.

by the extreme devotion of the younger generation, which, despite the persecutions, had ignited the ember of Judaism, and at the end of his visit he told Dr. Yitzhak Kogan, one of the Chabad movement's underground activists, that he would report back to the Rebbe what he had witnessed and ask him to especially bless Rabbi Yitzhak Kogan.

He was surprised to hear Rabbi Yitzhak ask that, instead of this, Rabbi Menachem Mendel should bless Yosef Mendelevich, a Prisoner of Zion who had been in prison already for ten years. Yosef had been arrested in Leningrad Airport together with his friends for attempting to hijack a Soviet plane and flee to Israel. 'He has currently been on a hunger strike for 55 days, demanding to give him back the Chumash and Siddur they confiscated from him,' said Yitzhak Kogan. 'His physical condition is very bad. The Rebbe must pray for his immediate release from the prison.'

And in fact the Rebbe's prayer was answered, and within a few months Yosef was flown straight from the prison to Israel. On a stopover in Vienna they brought the redeemed prisoner to the Israel Embassy in Austria. 'What is your first request?' the ambassador asked him. 'I need a set of Tefillin (phylacteries) to lay before sunset.' The Ambassador looked at his embassy staff members. Which of them would still have Tefillin? Suddenly there stepped forward Rabbi Israel Singer, the then Director of the World Jewish Congress. 'Very interesting,' said Singer. 'After hearing about the release of Mendelevich I was supposed to fly out to welcome him. Before that, I contacted Rabbi Menachem Mendel and asked him, what I should take for the freed Yosef?' 'Take him Tefillin,' said the Rebbe. 'And here are the Tefillin I have brought you on the orders of the Rebbe.' And so, for the first time in his life, Yosef put on the Tefillin. After he arrived in Israel, the Tefillin disappeared. Yosef was heartbroken.

Avraham Yitzchak Rahamim Mendelevich, one of Yosef's sons who was a student at the Carmiel Hesder Yeshiva, had been called up to serve in the IDF a year and eight months previously in an Armored Corps battalion. The commanders thought that he was ideal officer material, and pressed him to continue to serve. But Avraham Yitzchak (named after Rabbi Avraham Yitzchak HaCohen Kook) refused. 'I am going back to the yeshiva.'

On the day he was due to be released from the IDF, Operation Protective Edge began, and he was sent from the Golan Heights to fight in Gaza. His battalion was stationed on the outskirts of the Zaitoun neighborhood, not far from the settlement of Netzarim. Avraham Yitzchak very much regretted that he would not be able this year to go to the grave of his grandfather, Moshe Mendelevich, an Aliya activist in Riga in the 1970s, on his Yahrzeit, 16 Tammuz, the eve of the Three Weeks, the annual period of mourning for the Destruction of the Temple.

He did not know that, precisely on that day, the Tefillin which Rabbi Menachem Mendel had ordered to be given to his father Yosef, were found. It turned out that the Tefillin were with a nephew, Ronen Lisitzin.

The moment Yosef Mendelevich received the Tefillin back, he began to think how to get them to Avraham Yitzhak and give him special protection. However, it turned out that it was not possible to send the Tefillin to the battle area. But, as it is known, Hashem turns good intentions into deeds, and Yosef hoped that, thanks to all these things, the Tefillin would begin to perform their mission.

Contact with Avraham Yitzchak was very difficult. With the entry into the battle zone the phones were taken from the combatants. In brief sallies to the rear for equipping the tank with ammunition and for repairs, Avraham Yitzchak would contact his parents on the unit commander's phone. Every such conversation was a gift from Heaven and caused great excitement in the family. His mother asked her son to observe all the safety regulations and his father asked him to read Psalms from the Book of Tehillim every day.

In the zone where Battalion No. 7 was located, fierce battles were taking place. The terrorists were using anti-tank missiles as well as snipers and attacks from the tunnels. All of Am Israel prayed for the success of the soldiers and their safe return.

It happened on Rosh Hodesh Av, the new Hebrew month of Av. There was a powerful flash of light in the tank, followed by the sound of a huge explosion. The tank filled with smoke. Over the intercom they announced 'Tank No. 3 has been destroyed.' Avraham Yitzhak relates that his ears were deafened by the explosion. He didn't know whether he had been wounded and what had happened to his companions. A minute later he heard the commander shouting: 'Are you all alive?' They were all alive. At that moment they received the order to return fire and they scored a direct hit on the one who had fired the missile.

And this is how Avraham described the miracle that had occurred:

> There was a ceasefire, and we retreated to a safe position to rest. The commander gave us permission to leave the tank. We had spent 48 hours inside it, it was very hot, we were exhausted. But

I decided to remain in the tank. I had promised Father that I would read Tehillim every day and I had to read the Tehillim of Monday, Psalm 30... '1. A Psalm; a Song at the Dedication of the House; of David. 2. I will extol Thee, O Lord, for Thou hast raised me up, and hast not suffered mine enemies to rejoice over me.' And because I didn't go out, my fellow crew members also remained with me inside the tank.

Even though we were hidden inside an olive grove, the Hamas lookouts spotted us. They shot at us apparently with a Sagger guided anti-tank missile. In fact, there was no chance of escaping from this missile. But the Hamasnik and the missile struck exactly the rear of the tank. So, at first, they thought that we had been hit.

When the tank crew emerged from the tank, Avraham looked at the place in the tank turret where he was supposed to have stood during the rest period. All the equipment was burnt. The missile has passed one metre from the place.

At the thanksgiving meal which took place in his parents' home in Jerusalem, Avraham Yitzhak told about the miracle that had happened

Blessing the son of Russian immigrants to the United States after making a speech in Chicago, 2013.

Arriving with a Sefer Torah to demonstrate in Reykjavik for free Aliya immigration during the summit meeting between Reagan and Gorbachev in 1987.

to him thanks to the Guardian of Israel, and thanks to the Tehillim of King David. Then his father, Rabbi Yosef Mendelevich, stood up and told everyone about the Tehillim which the Rebbe had sent him 33 years previously, and which had turned up exactly during the current fighting.

Epilogue

THE PSALM OF DAVID

Many important things happened to me in my life.
I found the way to the truth.
I came out from darkness into the light.
I arrived in the Holy Land – Eretz Israel.
I studied Torah.

I built a home, and together with my wife, brought children and
grandchildren into the world.
And I am still continuing to discover many favors which Hashem has
bestowed on me.

I thank the Holy One Blessed Be He for the miracle He wrought with
me and with all the Jewish People, and continues to do so.

The special sense of rescue and revival is expressed by King David in
Chapter 30 of Psalms:

I will extol Thee, O Lord, for Thou has raised me up,
And hast not sufferd mine enemies to rejoice over me.
O Lord my God,
I cried unto Thee, and Thou didst heal me;
O Lord . Thou broughtest up my soul from the nether-world;
Thou didst keep me alive, that I should not go down to the pit.

Completed on the anniversary of the passing of my father, Moshe
Ben Aharon, 17 Tammuz.